ACADEMIC LIBRARIES
FOR COMMUTER STUDENTS

ACADEMIC LIBRARIES FOR COMMUTER STUDENTS

Research-Based Strategies

EDITED BY

MARIANA REGALADO

and

MAURA A. SMALE

ALA
Editions

CHICAGO | 2018

Extensive effort has gone into ensuring the reliability of the information in this book; however, the publisher makes no warranty, express or implied, with respect to the material contained herein.

ISBNs
978-0-8389-1701-5 (paper)
978-0-8389-1736-7 (PDF)
978-0-8389-1735-0 (ePub)
978-0-8389-1737-4 (Kindle)

Library of Congress Cataloging-in-Publication Data

Names: Regalado, Mariana, editor. | Smale, Maura A., editor.
Title: Academic libraries for commuter students : research-based strategies / edited by Mariana Regalado and Maura A. Smale.
Description: Chicago : ALA Editions, an imprint of the American Library Association, 2018. | Includes bibliographical references and index.
Identifiers: LCCN 2018003537| ISBN 9780838917015 (print : alk. paper) | ISBN 9780838917350 (epub) | ISBN 9780838917367 (pdf) | ISBN 9780838917374 (kindle)
Subjects: LCSH: Academic libraries—Services to commuting college students—United States. | Commuting college students—United States—Case studies. | Libraries and colleges—United States—Case studies.
Classification: LCC Z675.U5 A335 2018 | DDC 027.7—dc23 LC record available at https://lccn.loc.gov/2018003537

Cover design by Karen Sheets de Gracia. © Alexey Protasov/Adobe Stock. Text design in the Chaparral, Gotham, and Bell Gothic typefaces.

⊗ This paper meets the requirements of ANSI/NISO Z39.48-1992 (Permanence of Paper).

Printed in the United States of America

22 21 20 19 18   5 4 3 2 1

For my mother,
who has long been my model for the many pleasures
and satisfactions of collegial academic collaboration.
–M.R.

For Jonathan and Gus,
I was grateful to share workspace with you while
on sabbatical, and am grateful to share homespace
with you always.
–M.A.S.

Contents

Acknowledgments

ANY BOOK IS BY NECESSITY THE WORK OF MANY HANDS, and an edited volume inherently so. We'd like to thank our colleagues who contributed their work with commuter students to this volume; they graciously shared their fascinating projects with us, and cheerfully responded to our many e-mails about deadlines and other details. Their review of, and suggestions for, Chapters 1 and 9—especially Nancy Fried Foster, Tanner Wray, Ted Chodock, Sara Lowe, Brian Greene, and Elizabeth Horan—undoubtedly strengthened these chapters. Jill Cirasella and Jonathan Miller provided invaluable feedback on the chapter on the City University of New York (CUNY) we wrote with Jean Amaral, who is a thoughtful and smart collaborator. Continued interest in and support of our work from colleagues in our libraries, at CUNY, and beyond eased our way in successfully completing this project. Thank you!

MAURA A. SMALE and
MARIANA REGALADO

1

Situating Commuter Undergraduates

I t's a crisp fall morning as a New York City College of Technology student leaves her apartment in the Bronx to head to class in Brooklyn. Her commute takes nearly two hours and includes a short leg on the bus and a longer leg on the subway; while the morning rush hour can be crowded, she gets on the subway early enough in its route that she can usually get a seat. Some days she spends the commute just listening to music or reading for fun, though other days she'll review schoolwork on her smartphone, reading a screenshot she took of online course materials so she has access to them while the subway is underground.

Meanwhile, in North Carolina, a UNC Charlotte student gets ready to drive to campus for the day. Her commute takes about forty-five minutes door to door, and she parks on campus because she has paid the parking permit fee for the semester. Even with a permit the parking options on campus vary, and parking in part shapes the structure of her days. If she gets a parking place on the outskirts of campus, she'll sometimes use her long break between classes to run errands, but if she ends up with a good parking spot she tends to stay on campus for the day, studying in the library between classes.

Later that day, across the country in northern California, a Modesto Junior College student heads to work. He drives to commute between his work, school, home, and other responsibilities. While his commute isn't long, he makes the most of his time in the car by listening to audio recordings of his course readings while he drives, though he admits that this multitasking can be somewhat distracting. He fits in studying and homework when and where he can: at work during slow times, at the college library during class breaks (which he prefers for its distraction-free environment), and at home in the evenings after the library is closed.

■ ■ ■

Like these three undergraduates, the majority of American college students are commuters. While undergraduates who commute to campus are as diverse in their demographics as all college students, there are a number of important considerations specific to living off campus and commuting to school. Most notably, commuter students are much more likely than residential students to have responsibilities apart from their roles on campus. These responsibilities may be as basic as cooking their own meals, but they are also likely to include working full- or part-time, child care, family or community obligations, and more. Students who live off campus often must negotiate living spaces with family, roommates, or others outside of the learning institution. Moreover, the mode of each student's commute may deeply impact her days, and possibly involve a considerable time commitment. Yet, despite the large numbers of commuter students in the United States, and the complexities of their lives, there is a need for research and publications on the "overlooked majority" of commuter college students (Biddix 2015; Dugan et al. 2008), and, specifically, on how academic libraries serve this population.

In this volume we bring together studies undertaken by librarians and researchers at community and baccalaureate colleges and universities from locations across the United States, covering commuter institutions and those with both commuter and residential populations. Each chapter is a case study of research on serving commuter students at a particular institution, encompassing a detailed description of the research methods used, analysis of what was learned during the research, and specific interventions or changes made in library services, resources, or facilities as a result. Taking into account the lived experiences of commuter students at our institutions can enable librarians to design and develop services, resources, and facilities to best meet the needs of these students.

DEFINING UNDERGRADUATE COMMUTER STUDENTS

Contrary to the popular view of "traditional" college students—those who are between 18 and 24 years old and who live in dormitories or residence halls on their college or university campus—the National Center for Education Statistics (NCES) reports that close to 87 percent of students at U.S. colleges and universities are commuters (NCES 2012). Yet, while most students commute, they have not been the focus of research studies to the same degree as have "traditional" students. There is no single definition of commuter college students; rather, the broad category of "commuter" incorporates a wide range of attributes and many nuances, as the case studies in this volume explore.

The NCES subdivides the commuter student population into those who live off campus with their parents, just under 37 percent, and those who live off campus but not with their parents—about 50 percent of all undergraduates (NCES 2012). However, these categories do not encompass all of the potential variation in commuter students' living arrangements. Students may live in campus housing for their first year before moving to housing that is not owned by the university, though remaining close to campus. Others may live in residence halls that are owned by the institution but are far enough away from the main areas of campus to require a commute by car or bus. Students who live off campus may live with roommates or with extended family. For the purposes of this discussion, commuters are students who do not live in college-provided housing on campus, for them, "home" is a place independent from the institution, no matter what their physical distance from the institution is.

The National Survey of Student Engagement (NSSE) further differentiates between commuters who walk to campus and those who drive (Jacoby 2015a, 290). Yet this distinction does not take into account differences in commuting to colleges in urban, suburban, and rural areas, including transit times. In urban areas, where more American undergraduates attend college than in all suburban and rural areas combined (Florida 2016), reliance on public transportation may supersede the distinction between walking or driving to campus (Clark 2006, 3). Suburban students or those on physically large campuses may also rely on intra-campus or public buses, especially if they cannot afford to drive; other transportation options include carpooling, car-sharing, or bicycling. Intriguingly, recent research suggests that many students do not consider those who live close enough to campus to walk there to fit into the category of "commuters" (Badger 2014). The cost and reliability of transportation can seriously affect students' opportunities to participate in their academic commitments (Jacoby 2015a, 292). Indeed, understanding students' commutes is highly relevant to their experiences in our institutions (Clark 2006; Delcore, Mullooly, and Scroggins 2009).

Adding further to this complexity, commuter students are typically found to share at least some of the characteristics of nontraditional college students (Jacoby 2015a, 290; Newbold, Mehta, and Forbus 2011), who are defined as

> being independent for financial aid purposes, having one or more dependents, being a single caregiver, not having a traditional high school diploma, delaying postsecondary enrollment, attending school part time, and being employed full time. (NCES 2015, 1)

While there is overlap between the categories of commuter and nontraditional students, considering them as coterminous elides their distinctions. For example, most students work for pay at some point in college, though not all students work full-time (Alfano and Eduljee 2013). Furthermore, students at predominantly or solely commuter institutions may share a majority of characteristics with their "traditional" peers at residential campuses, such as age (18–24), work status (part-time or not at all), and enrollment status (full-time).

However, many commuter students have responsibilities outside of their academic work, sometimes quite significant and time-consuming ones (Burlison 2015; Perna 2010). They may work part-time or full-time, and it is likely that their jobs are off campus. They may care for children, siblings, parents, or other family members. Commuters who remain in their homes and communities are more likely to retain involvement in nonacademic activities in these locations, such as participating in religious communities, volunteer work, or other community commitments. These activities are often valued by students, but may constrain their time available for on-campus commitments beyond their coursework.

Institutions with a majority of residential students may not be as welcoming to their commuter students, since "facilities, class schedules, and campus life are still frequently designed to suit traditional-age, full-time, often residential students" (Jacoby 2015b, 9). Even those colleges and universities in which most or all students commute may lack accommodations that could benefit commuter students specifically; for example, clustering required courses to reduce the number of days on which students must come to campus, or offering facilities and services specifically for students who cannot return to their homes during the school day or who are primarily on campus on evenings and weekends. Considering support networks for commuter students—both on campus and in students' lives outside of the institution—as well as advisement and orientation for commuter students can help ameliorate their marginality (Jacoby and Garland 2004). While the chapters in this volume explore the ways in which academic libraries can support commuter students, it is useful to consider previous case studies on the commuter student experience.

RESEARCH ON THE COMMUTER STUDENT EXPERIENCE

Since commuters are such a large percentage of college students overall, examining research on them can add context to inform our understanding of the spaces, resources, instruction, and other services that academic libraries provide. Much published research has focused on commuters who are in the minority of students enrolled at predominantly residential institutions. Overall, literature on the experiences of commuter undergraduates is primarily concerned with discussion of student engagement and academic success.

Student Engagement and Academic Success

Student engagement has been shown to positively impact the standard measures of student success, including grade point average (GPA), year-to-year retention rate (also referred to as academic persistence), and graduation rate. As defined by the NSSE, student engagement includes both "the amount of time and effort" students spend on academics as well as "how the institution deploys its resources" to provide students with opportunities "to participate in activities that decades of research studies show are linked to student learning" (NSSE 2017).

Nearly two decades ago, Jacoby (2000b, 4) expressed concern about commuter students' involvement in their education, since "uninvolved students tend to not study enough, spend little time on campus, not be involved in student life, and have few contacts with faculty and fellow students." She further suggested that, despite educational goals that "are just as high as those of residential students," commuters "simply cannot always make education their primary focus" (5). Kuh, Gonyea, and Palmer (2001, 1) reiterated that commuters are less involved in college life than residential students "who go away to college," and that commuters are "distracted by too many competing demands on their time because of work or family commitments." Using NSSE data, these authors concluded that "residential students were more engaged in effective educational practices and—in all likelihood—were benefiting more from their college experience" than were commuter students (6).

While Kuh, Gonyea, and Palmer (2001, 9) acknowledged that "the effect sizes are relatively small" in their research, the sense of commuter students as a population of concern within undergraduate institutions persists. While commuter students clearly have different attributes and needs than their residential peers, the continued framing of commuter students as a problem in need of fixing has permeated much research in the past two decades, despite many changes in higher education during that time. More recent research has begun to complicate and extend the picture of commuter students' experiences.

A survey of students at a private college with a mixed commuter and residential population found that participation in extracurricular activities was lower for commuters than for residential students, and more commuters than residential students wished they were more connected with campus life, though some residential students wished for more connection as well (Alfano and Eduljee 2013). Institutional research at a large, predominantly commuter university revealed that in-state and Hispanic students were more likely to be commuters, while black students and those of higher socioeconomic status were more likely to be residential. However, no significant difference was found for GPA and other academic success measures between commuter and residential students (Gianoutsos and Rosser 2014). Researchers who examined NCES data have also found that commuting had no significant effect on student persistence from the first to second year (Ishitani and Reid 2015, 22).

Finally, a survey at a large university examined commuters and distance traveled and found no evidence that living farther away from campus impacted students' GPA (Nelson et al. 2016).

A 2016 study using NSSE data to specifically examine living environments and student engagement significantly updates our understanding of the commuter student experience (Gonyea, Hurtado, and Graham 2017). This research found "subdued" effects of students' living environment on a range of measures. While there was a positive effect for residential students on retention and graduation, there were negative effects on residential students' psychological well-being in the first year especially, and inconclusive effects on cognitive outcomes, diversity attitudes, and academic self-concept. The researchers posit that commuter students in general are more engaged than in the past, and note that previous research did not account for the nuances between residential and commuter student experiences. They concluded by asserting that if "institutions have made headway in integrating off campus students into the academic and social community, then the benefits of living on campus have not declined, rather the ill-effects of living off campus have been attenuated" (21).

Student Identity and Multiple Life Roles

Several studies have examined identity in commuter undergraduates. A qualitative study by Clark (2005) at an urban commuter college highlighted students' inexperience with their roles as college students. This unfamiliarity prevented students from strategizing effectively; she suggested that "common experiences" and a focus on finding time and space to study can be effective ways to help students be successful. A survey of commuter students at a university with a mixed commuter and residential population disclosed that commuters were more likely to be nontraditional students, worked more hours than residential students, and were less likely to participate in campus activities than residential students, confirming prior research (Newbold, Mehta, and Forbus 2011, 149). Results from a focus group and survey at a university with both residential and commuter students focused on "the sources of [commuter students'] stress with college life and the coping strategies they employ" (Forbus, Newbold, and Mehta 2010). They found that while commuter students did report more stress, they had developed more effective strategies to deal with stress than had residential students.

A focus on commuter students' identities and multiple life roles includes several studies that specifically examined aspects of student engagement. Research using NSSE results found higher engagement levels for black students at an urban commuter university who were involved in Greek organizations, interacted often with faculty, and participated in cocurricular activities (Yearwood and Jones 2012). Studies at a private college and urban public university with mixed residential and commuter enrollment explored living situations and family commitments that commuter students may have in addition to their required coursework. Findings revealed that students perceive the support and understanding of their families to be important to their success, though a lack of family adaptation to a student's academic role could be a challenge (Burlison 2015, 30; see also Badger 2014). A survey of freshman student adjustment at an urban commuter college also had mixed results: student athletes found it easier to adjust to the social component of college, while women had an easier time adjusting to the academics of college than men (Melendez 2016).

Research on faculty perceptions of the experience of commuter students is also relevant to the study of commuter students' experiences. Focus group research conducted with faculty at two commuter universities and a community college suggested that faculty understood that working commuter students have multiple life roles (Ziskin, Zerquera, and Torres 2010, 11), realized the many challenges of working students, and knew about student strategies and their lives (Zerquera, Ziskin, and Torres 2016). Interviews conducted with faculty at several urban commuter colleges revealed similar insights (Smale and Regalado 2014). Interestingly, while faculty acknowledge that students "compartmentalize these roles, . . . findings also suggest that these faculty and practitioners believe students *should* compartmentalize their multiple roles to promote their academic success" (Ziskin, Zerquera, and Torres 2010, 11, emphasis added). Further, most of the faculty interviewed had a traditional college experience themselves, which required them to adapt their understanding of their students' lives (12).

Students and the Commute

The student experience while commuting has also been the focus of a few studies. In interviews with urban students who use public transportation, researchers found that many students were eager to take advantage of commute time for schoolwork, though the realities of crowded buses and subway cars could make this difficult (Regalado and Smale 2015a). These students were more likely to engage in reading or writing than the average urban public transit commuter (Lopatovska et al. 2011). Latino commuter students interviewed at a large university shared their concerns about "the high level of traffic, taking the bus to school, and the amount of time and energy involved in commuting to campus" (Hernandez 2002, 75). A study of the scholarly activities of undergraduates in suburban California found that they often used their cars as private study spaces while on campus (Delcore, Mullooly, and Scroggins 2009). Other studies of students who drive to campus have found high levels of stress among students who drive, stress that is related to traffic and the need to find parking in particular (Forbus, Newbold, and Mehta 2010).

Technology and Commuter Students

Though technology is especially relevant to academic libraries, research on commuter student experiences has not explored the impact of technology on higher education, especially the development of the Internet, instructional technology, and personal mobile devices like smartphones. Some scholars have suggested that technology might be used to increase the amount of contact between faculty and commuter students, both to "create academic community" and to increase "student learning outside the curriculum" (Kruger 2000, 66) and between the institution and commuter students, especially by using social media to promote programs and events and to provide useful information (Yearwood and Jones 2012, 122). Recent surveys of U.S. college students' technology use reveal that undergraduates own more computing devices than does the population as a whole, and that they "use their devices extensively and view them as important to their academic success" (Brooks 2016, 5). Other studies found that students "prefer courses that use technology" (Buckenmeyer et al. 2016), and that commuters in particular rely on their smartphones to complete schoolwork while in transit (Smale and Regalado 2017). Ultimately, many hope that technology may be used to increase commuter students' engagement with the institution (Kretovics 2015; Yearwood and Jones 2012). However, it is important to note the persistence of the digital divide in the United States: smartphone ownership and home broadband access decrease along with household income, and in 2016 only 64 percent of those with household incomes of less than $30,000 a year owned a smartphone (Rainie 2017). This unequal access may hinder commuter students especially.

COMMUTER STUDENTS IN ACADEMIC LIBRARIES

Understanding the practices of commuter students in college and university libraries is critical to planning and deploying resources and services to meet their needs. Previous research on commuter students in the academic library literature has centered on three themes: the library as place, studies of information literacy and library instruction for commuter students, and technology that commuter students use for their academic work.

A number of studies have acknowledged the important role that academic libraries play as a place for student work on campus, and have sought to understand how commuters use their academic libraries in order to better serve those students. Some have focused on or revealed insight into subgroups of the commuter student population. Qualitative research with Hispanic students at an urban university revealed that they "are trying to balance work and school, spend significant time commuting, and have limited access to quiet space for studying"; they highly valued the library as a study location

(Green 2012, 97). A recent study using ethnographic methods at a small, urban, primarily commuter college at which a majority of students are black and female found that commuter students appreciated the library as a place to build community, though they acknowledged the tension between collaborative work and the need for quiet work space (Manley 2015). Research at an urban commuter college examined student use of the 24-hour study space, a new service offered during finals week, and learned that the heaviest users of the study space tended to be younger and full-time students early in their college careers who lived with their parents (Richards 2016, 11).

Other research has examined multiple institutions and libraries revealing both specific, local needs as well as common themes. Using surveys and seating sweeps, researchers in five Canadian academic libraries with a mix of commuter and residential populations suggested that "students perceive the combination of setting, resources, and community that the library provides as an incubator for learning and that, by virtue of being among these things, they believe they will learn" (May and Swabey 2015, 790); this is congruent with findings from other studies (Khoo et al. 2016; Regalado and Smale 2015b). Research at an urban library that serves three predominantly commuter colleges also highlighted the centrality of library resources and services to their academic work; students requested more computers and more quiet space for studying (Brown-Sica 2012). A study of five regional, solely commuter campuses of a state university system created a survey to learn more about the specific needs of each regional campus (Dryden and Roseman 2010). Importantly, some of these researchers were able to leverage their data to create renovation plans or add services to better meet the needs of their commuter students (Dryden and Roseman 2010; Brown-Sica 2012; Richards 2016).

While information literacy and library instruction is a heavily researched topic in academic libraries, there are few studies of information literacy specifically for commuter college and university students. Studies on library instruction at community colleges partially fill this gap, since the overwhelming majority of community college students are commuters rather than residential students. A review of the literature on the information needs of mature—that is, over age twenty-four—community college students reveals that they bring a range of prior experiences with libraries and information literacy (Zeit 2014). These authors suggest that a focus on the unique needs of these students, especially for those who don't plan to go on to seek a baccalaureate degree, can contribute to their success in college and in their careers.

In recent years there has been an increasing focus on technology for information literacy and library instruction, and the use of technology more generally to support all students in academic libraries. Librarians at an urban commuter college note that commuter students rely heavily on mobile devices for their academic work, both on and off campus and on the commute. In order to accommodate and support these students, they began to offer library instruction specifically focused on using mobile devices to access the library and do research (Havelka and Verbovetskaya 2012). Much has been written about library support for online learning, and commuter students share some attributes of distance-learning students as well: they may have limited time on campus or fit their homework into times in their schedule when the library is closed, and thus may benefit from increased online access to library resources and services. Research on strategies to engage distance-learning students with the library—such as online reference available twenty-four hours a day, online tutorials and research guides, and embedding librarians into course websites or learning management systems—may also be relevant to commuter students in college and university libraries (Hedreen 2012).

ABOUT THIS BOOK

This book aims to make a significant contribution to the academic library literature by focusing specifically on research with commuter students, in order to help academic librarians understand the unique needs of commuters and contribute to their success in college. We have sought here to include a wide range of U.S. colleges and universities that serve commuter students. Institutions large and small from urban and suburban locations all over the country are represented. Some are solely (or almost solely) commuter campuses, while others serve a mix of commuter and residential students in varying proportions; flagship, regional, and single-campus institutions are included. The transportation that students use to attend these colleges and universities also varies, from driving with its attendant need for parking, to public transportation like buses, subways, or regional rail, to bicycling or walking. Housing situations—determined in large part by the cost of living in a particular area—differ for students between and within these institutions, as does the availability of other spaces for students to engage in academic work, such as public libraries, their jobs, cafes, and parks, among others. These variations in space availability have an impact on commuter students that may not be felt among their residential counterparts. The studies in this book further seek to complement and complicate existing research on commuter students. Many of the researchers use qualitative methods of data collection and analysis, or a mix of qualitative and quantitative methods, which provide different insight into the lived experiences of commuter students than the primarily quantitative research published in the higher education literature (Badger 2014).

The chapters in this volume present case studies of research on commuter students at college and university libraries. The chapters are organized by institution type, beginning with large universities with some residential students, and moving on to institutions that almost exclusively enroll commuter students, most of which are community colleges. All chapter authors explain the research question or aim of the research project and describe the institutional context, with special consideration of the needs of commuter and residential students for institutions that serve both. In addition to sharing the results of their research, chapter authors discuss what was learned during their studies with a focus on specific interventions or initiatives that have been undertaken (or are planned) in their libraries to better serve commuter students. Authors describe the research methods used in detail so that readers may replicate the research at their own institutions if desired.

In chapter 2, M. Sara Lowe, Willie Miller, and Paul Moffett share their work on two space assessment projects at the main library at Indiana University-Purdue University Indianapolis (IUPUI). Traditionally a commuter campus, IUPUI has substantially increased the number of residential students in the last decade, which has introduced new patterns of library use. Using both qualitative and quantitative methods, their research revealed important ways that the library could move ahead to best meet the changing needs of both populations of students.

Donna Lanclos and Rachael Winterling discuss the implementation of the Family Friendly Library Room at the University of North Carolina, Charlotte, in chapter 3. This innovative library space is intended to address the unique needs of commuter students and their children. This chapter demonstrates how the project was grounded in prior space-use studies and an initial assessment of student needs. Subsequent interviews with students about how they actually used the room provided critical information for assessing the project's successes and suggesting areas for improvement.

Chapter 4, by Juliann Couture, brings us to the University of Colorado Boulder, where mapping and interviews were used to learn more about the lived experiences of students who often begin their college careers in campus housing and then move off campus. This research has helped interrogate the place of the library within the "campus bubble" that defines much of the student experience on this large public university's flagship campus, and has informed space planning decisions.

In chapter 5, Jean Amaral, Mariana Regalado, and Maura Smale discuss their qualitative research with students at seven colleges of the City University of New York (CUNY), the largest urban public university in the United States and a predominantly commuter institution. Incorporating both community colleges and four-year schools and spanning nearly a decade, their research projects have explored the experiences and frustrations of this diverse student body. In particular, this research illuminates strategies for completing academic work among urban students who primarily commute via public transportation.

Chapters 6 through 8 present research from community colleges in the United States, a population that is not well studied even though 45 percent of U.S. undergraduates attend a community college (American Association of Community Colleges 2016). Most, though not all, community colleges do not offer campus housing, thus community college students make up a large proportion of commuter undergraduates in the United States.

In chapter 6, Brian Greene and Elizabeth Horan examine the lived experiences of students at Modesto Junior College in northern California and Coastline Community College in southern California. Both are community colleges, yet they differ in location and the prevalence of online learning at each institution. Research into the nonacademic commitments of students, their living situations, and transportation requirements revealed much about student study habits, and suggests strategies that both libraries—despite their differences—can implement to better serve their students.

In chapter 7, Tanner Wray and Nancy Fried Foster share research into the place of the library in the student experience at the three campuses of Montgomery College in Maryland. This large study involved participation from multiple stakeholders across all three campuses to learn about student academic work practices and faculty and staff experiences in the libraries and beyond, and has illuminated the differing needs of each campus while leading to a more solid embedding of the libraries into the life of this community college.

Chapter 8, by Ted Chodock, discusses the assessment of instruction and information literacy at the College of Southern Nevada, a highly diverse community college in the Las Vegas metropolitan area. Drawing on research performed as a participant in the Association of College & Research Libraries' Assessment in Action program, this chapter explores the effect of student engagement in different types of library instruction on student success outcomes.

We conclude the volume in chapter 9 by bringing together insights gained from the research studies included here and suggestions for future research. We have learned about the centrality of the commute to students' lives, the importance of place on campus for commuter students, the value of collaborating within and beyond the library, and the benefits of listening to students' experiences and ideas. We hope that readers not only find the information shared in this volume to be useful in their own practice as academic librarians, but are also inspired to learn more about their own commuter students.

REFERENCES

Alfano, Halley J., and Nina B. Eduljee. 2013. "Differences in Work, Levels of Involvement, and Academic Performance between Residential and Commuter Students." *College Student Journal* 47 (2): 334–42.

American Association of Community Colleges. 2016. "Fast Facts from Our Fact Sheet." www.aacc.nche.edu/AboutCC/Pages/fastfactsfactsheet.aspx.

Badger, Caitlin W. 2014. "A Student Perspective: Commuter Student Experiences, Definitions and Self-Identification." *Humphrey Public Affairs Review.* http://humphreyreview.umn.edu/student-perspective-commuter-student-experiences-definitions-and-self-identification.

Biddix, J. Patrick. 2015. "Editor's Notes." *New Directions for Student Services* 2015 (150): 1–2. doi:10.1002/ss.20121.

Brooks, D. Christopher. 2016. *ECAR Study of Undergraduate Students and Information Technology, 2016.* Louisville, CO: ECAR. https://library.educause.edu/resources/2016/6/2016-students-and-technology-research-study.

Brown-Sica, Margaret S. 2012. "Library Spaces for Urban, Diverse Commuter Students: A Participatory Action Research Project." *College & Research Libraries* 73 (3): 217–31. doi:10.5860/crl-221.

Buckenmeyer, Janet A., Casimir Barczyk, Emily Hixon, Heather Zamojski, and Annette Tomory. 2016. "Technology's Role in Learning at a Commuter Campus: The Student Perspective." *Journal of Further and Higher Education* 40 (3): 412–31. doi:10.1080/0309877X.2014.984596.

Burlison, Mary Beth. 2015. "Nonacademic Commitments Affecting Commuter Student Involvement and Engagement." *New Directions for Student Services* 2015 (150): 27–34. doi:10.1002/ss.20124.

Clark, Marcia Roe. 2005. "Negotiating the Freshman Year: Challenges and Strategies among First-Year College Students." *Journal of College Student Development* 46 (3): 296–316. doi:10.1353/csd.2005.0022.

———. 2006. "Succeeding in the City: Challenges and Best Practices on Urban Commuter Campuses." *About Campus* 11 (3): 2–8. doi:10.1002/abc.166.

Delcore, Henry D., James Mullooly, and Michael Scroggins. 2009. *The Library Study at Fresno State.* Fresno, CA: Institute of Public Anthropology, California State University. www.csufresno.edu/anthropology/ipa/thelibrarystudy.html.

Dryden, Nancy H., and Shelley G. Roseman. 2010. "Learning Commons: Addressing the Needs of Commuter Regional Campuses." *Journal of Library Administration* 50 (5–6): 581–601. doi:10.1080/01930826.2010.488917.

Dugan, John P., John L. Garland, Barbara Jacoby, and Anna Gasiorski. 2008. "Understanding Commuter Student Self-Efficacy for Leadership: A Within-Group Analysis." *NASPA Journal* 45 (2): 282–310. doi:10.2202/1949–6605.1951.

Florida, Richard. 2016. "America's Biggest College Towns." CityLab. September 8. www.citylab.com/housing/2016/09/americas-biggest-college-towns/498755/.

Forbus, Patricia, John Newbold, and Sanjay Mehta. 2010. "University Commuter Students: Time Management, Stress Factors and Coping Strategies." *Advances in Business Research* 1 (1): 142–51.

Gianoutsos, D., and Vicki Rosser. 2014. "Is There 'Still' a Considerable Difference? Comparing Residential and Commuter Student Profile Characteristics at a Public, Research, Commuter University." *College Student Journal* 48 (4): 613–28.

Gonyea, Robert M., Sarah S. Hurtado, and Polly A. Graham. 2017. "Living Environments and Student Engagement: Research Findings and Implications." Presentation at the American College Personnel Association Annual Convention, March 26–29, Columbus, OH. http://nsse.indiana.edu/pdf/presentations/2017/ACPA_2017_Gonyea_Hurtado_Graham_slides.pdf.

Green, David. 2012. "Supporting the Academic Success of Hispanic Students." In *College Libraries and Student Culture: What We Now Know,* edited by Lynda M. Duke and Andrew D. Asher, 87–108. Chicago: American Library Association.

Havelka, Stefanie, and Alevtina Verbovetskaya. 2012. "Mobile Information Literacy: Let's Use an App for That!" *College & Research Libraries News* 73 (1): 22–23. http://crln.acrl.org/index.php/crlnews/article/view/8689.

Hedreen, Rebecca. 2012. "Time Zones, Screencasts, and Becoming Real: Lessons Learned as a Distance Librarian." *Urban Library Journal* 18 (1). http://academicworks.cuny.edu/ulj/v0118/iss1/3.

Hernandez, John C. 2002. "A Qualitative Exploration of the First-Year Experience of Latino College Students." *NASPA Journal* 40 (1): 69–84. doi:10.2202/1949-6605.1189.

Ishitani, Terry T., and Aileen M. Reid. 2015. "First-to-Second-Year Persistence Profile of Commuter Students." *New Directions for Student Services* 2015 (150): 13–26. doi:10.1002/ss.20123.

Jacoby, Barbara. 2000a. *Involving Commuter Students in Learning.* San Francisco: Jossey-Bass.

———. 2000b. "Why Involve Commuter Students in Learning?" In *Involving Commuter Students in Learning,* edited by Barbara Jacoby, 3–12. San Francisco: Jossey-Bass.

———. 2015a. "Engaging Commuter and Part-Time Students." In *Student Engagement in Higher Education: Theoretical Perspectives and Practical Approaches for Diverse Populations,* edited by Stephen John Quaye and Shaun R. Harper, 2nd ed., 289–305. New York: Routledge.

———. 2015b. "Enhancing Commuter Student Success: What's Theory Got to Do with It?" *New Directions for Student Services* 2015 (150): 3–12. doi:10.1002/ss.20122.

Jacoby, Barbara, and John Garland. 2004. "Strategies for Enhancing Commuter Student Success." *Journal of College Student Retention: Research, Theory & Practice* 6 (1): 61–79. doi:10.2190/567C-5TME-Q8F4–8FRG.

Khoo, Michael J., Lily Rozaklis, Catherine Hall, and Diana Kusunoki. 2016. "'A Really Nice Spot': Evaluating Place, Space, and Technology in Academic Libraries." *College & Research Libraries* 77 (1): 51–70. doi:10.5860/crl.77.1.51.

Kretovics, Mark. 2015. "Commuter Students, Online Services, and Online Communities." *New Directions for Student Services* 2015 (150): 69–78. doi:10.1002/ss.20128.

Kruger, Kevin. 2000. "Using Information Technology to Create Communities of Learners." In *Involving Commuter Students in Learning,* edited by Barbara Jacoby, 59–70. San Francisco: Jossey-Bass.

Kuh, George D., Robert M. Gonyea, and Megan Palmer. 2001. "The Disengaged Commuter Student: Fact or Fiction?" *Commuter Perspectives* 27 (1): 2–5.

Lopatovska, Irene, Alexandra S. Basen, Anshuman D. Duneja, Helen Kwong, Denise L. Pasquinelli, Sarah Sopab, Brian M. Stokes, and Christopher Weller. 2011. "Information Behaviour of New York City Subway Commuters." *Information Research* 16 (4). http://informationr.net/ir/16–4/paper501.html.

Manley, Laura. 2015. *Building Community in the Academic Library: Exploring the Commuter Student Experience.* River Forest, IL: Dominican University. http://dom.constellation.libras.org/handle/10969/898.

May, Francine, and Alice Swabey. 2015. "Using and Experiencing the Academic Library: A Multisite Observational Study of Space and Place." *College & Research Libraries* 76 (6): 771–95. doi:10.5860/crl.76.6.771.

Melendez, Mickey C. 2016. "Adjustment to College in an Urban Commuter Setting: The Impact of Gender, Race/Ethnicity, and Athletic Participation." *Journal of College Student Retention: Research, Theory & Practice* 18 (1): 31–48. doi:10.1177/1521025115579671.

National Center for Education Statistics. 2012. "College & Career Tables Library." https://nces.ed.gov/datalab/tableslibrary/viewtable.aspx?tableid=9562.

———. 2015. "Demographic and Enrollment Characteristics of Nontraditional Undergraduates: 2011–12." Washington, DC. http://nces.ed.gov/pubsearch/pubsinfo.asp?pubid=2015025.

National Survey of Student Engagement. 2017. "About NSSE." http://nsse.indiana.edu/html/about.cfm.

Nelson, Danielle, Kaustav Misra, Gail E. Sype, and Wayne Mackie. 2016. "An Analysis of the Relationship between Distance from Campus and GPA of Commuter Students." *Journal of International Education Research* 12 (1): 37–46. doi:10.19030/jier.v12i1.9565.

Newbold, John J., Sanjay S. Mehta, and Patricia Forbus. 2011. "Commuter Students: Involvement and Identification with an Institution of Higher Education." *Academy of Educational Leadership Journal* 15 (2): 141–53.

Perna, Laura W., ed. 2010. *Understanding the Working College Student: New Research and Its Implications for Policy and Practice.* Sterling, VA: Stylus.

Rainie, Lee. 2017. "Digital Divides—Feeding America." Pew Research Center: Internet, Science & Tech. February 9. www.pewinternet.org/2017/02/09/digital-divides-feeding-america/.

Regalado, Mariana, and Maura A. Smale. 2015a. "Serving the Commuter College Student in Urban Academic Libraries." *Urban Library Journal* 21 (1). http://academicworks.cuny.edu/ulj/v0121/iss1/3.

———. 2015b. "'I Am More Productive in the Library Because It's Quiet': Commuter Students in the College Library." *College & Research Libraries* 76 (7): 899–913. doi:10.5860/crl.76.7.899.

Richards, Maureen. 2016. "24/7 Library Hours at an Urban Commuter College." *Urban Library Journal* 22 (1). http://academicworks.cuny.edu/ulj/v0122/iss1/2.

Smale, Maura A., and Mariana Regalado. 2014. "Commuter Students Using Technology." *EDUCAUSE Review Online,* September. http://er.educause.edu/articles/2014/9/commuter-students-using-technology.

———. 2017. *Digital Technology as Affordance and Barrier in Higher Education.* New York: Palgrave Macmillan.

Yearwood, Trina Lynn, and Elizabeth A. Jones. 2012. "Understanding What Influences Successful Black Commuter Students' Engagement in College." *The Journal of General Education* 61 (2): 97–125. doi:10.1353/jge.2012.0015.

Zeit, Krystina. 2014. "The Information Needs and Behavior of Mature Community College Students: A Review of Literature." *Community & Junior College Libraries* 20 (3–4): 57–62. doi:10.1080/02763915.2014.1015341.

Zerquera, Desiree D., Mary Ziskin, and Vasti Torres. 2016. "Faculty Views of 'Nontraditional' Students: Aligning Perspectives for Student Success." *Journal of College Student Retention: Research, Theory & Practice.* doi:10.1177/1521025116645109.

Ziskin, Mary, Desiree Zerquera, and Vasti Torres. 2010. "Faculty & Practitioners' Views of Working, Commuting Students: Aligning Perspectives for Academic Success." Project on Academic Success, Center for Postsecondary Research at Indiana University. http://pas.indiana.edu/pdf/ASHE2010_MWSC_PrFac.pdf.

M. SARA LOWE,
WILLIE MILLER, and
PAUL MOFFETT

2

Commuter Campus in Transition

Meeting the Changing Needs of Students through Mixed-Methods Assessment

Indiana University-Purdue University Indianapolis (IUPUI) is an urban research university with approximately 30,000 commuter and residential students. In 2015, the library administration was successful in gathering campus support for the first large-scale renovation of the University Library (UL) since its construction in 1993. In the years since it opened, the IUPUI campus and its student body have changed dramatically. The number of full-time students has increased by nearly 8,800 (69.9 percent), and the average freshman SAT score has increased by 182 points. The number of students living on campus increased from 350 in 2003 to more than 2,000 in 2014 (IUPUI 2014).

Although IUPUI has historically been a commuter campus, the student body is moving toward more traditionally aged, residential students. This shift is due in part to an IUPUI Strategic Plan initiative called Promote Undergraduate Student Learning and Success that includes increasing retention and grades and decreasing time to graduation (IUPUI 2017). The IUPUI administration has cited national studies which indicate that students who live on campus get better grades and have higher graduation rates (see, e.g., de Araujo and Murray 2010; National Survey of Student Engagement 2017). Under the eleven-year tenure of Chancellor Charles Bantz, IUPUI student life has greatly expanded as seen in the construction of the Campus Center, new student housing facilities, and the IUPUI Honors College (IUPUI 2014).

For UL, the shift from primarily commuter students to a mix of commuter and residential students poses a challenge when considering space needs. Residential students may move in and out of the library throughout their day or want longer library hours because they live on campus; commuter students may need computer access (rather than carrying around a laptop all day) and a place to study for an extended period of time between classes. While the student body changed, the library was not well positioned to change with it. Student study space is primarily located on the third and fourth floors of the library's four-story building; however, that space was originally designed as open stacks, with little space devoted to study furniture.

Because of the shift in enrollment, increasing student study space became the top priority for UL staff. Library administrators asked for a renovation to increase the quality and amount of student study space, enhance wayfinding, augment access to electric power, and upgrade the quality of library furniture. The IUPUI campus administration responded by funding a project to renovate the third and fourth floors of the library.

Librarians collected data on UL in the hope that it would empower the design team to preserve the functionality and success of existing study spaces, while also expanding on or introducing new features that students found important, useful, and inspiring. Furthermore, library staff would also be able to use the data to establish a benchmark for space usage that could be compared to data gathered after the renovation.

Two studies, started separately but later merged, have provided information about students' use of library space. They have aided librarians in identifying critical features that students value in library and non-library study spaces to include in the renovation planning. The studies combine quantitative and qualitative elements and different methodologies. The first was a smaller ($n = 27$) mapping study using SMS (texting) in combination with one-on-one debriefs to track student movement over the course of an entire day. The second used an in-library assessment to quantify student space use ($n = 10,076$). By combining in-library and out-of-library studies, UL can better plan library space, not only for current users, but also for students who are not in the library (non-users). These studies were intended to help campus architects and designers understand the student experience in the IUPUI University Library, especially as it differed from other libraries in the Indiana University (IU) system. In recent years, IU has renovated several libraries. The Herman B. Wells Library on the Bloomington campus, in Bloomington, Indiana, a traditional residential campus in a rural setting, was the latest library to be renovated. UL staff wanted to ensure that UL was considered in its context, as an urban campus with a mix of commuter and residential students. UL hoped the studies would provide data to help the space meet the needs of both types of students.

INSTITUTIONAL CONTEXT

IUPUI is located near the center of downtown Indianapolis, which is the fifteenth largest city in the United States (Evans 2017). Approximately 70 percent of the university's 30,000 students are undergraduates, with the other 30 percent in graduate or professional programs. Seventy-three percent of students attend IUPUI full-time (IUPUI Institutional Research and Decision Support 2017b). A majority of students come from the county in which IUPUI is located (Marion) or the four counties on each side (Hendricks, Hamilton, Johnson, and Hancock). For example, in Spring 2017, 60 percent of students came from one of these five counties: 33 percent from Marion County, and 27 percent from the four surrounding counties (IUPUI Institutional Research and Decision Support 2017c). As of 2015, 32 percent of undergraduates were the first in their family to attend college, and 14 percent of the student body was international (Dace et al. 2016). Regarding race, IUPUI is a relatively diverse campus, with 68 percent of students identifying as white, 9 percent black, 7 percent international, 6 percent Hispanic/Latino, 5 percent Asian, and 4 percent two or more races (IUPUI Housing and Residence Life 2017b).

In 2007, about 8 percent of first-time, full-time beginner students lived in campus housing, compared with 91 percent who did not. By 2016 that percentage had risen dramatically, and almost 49 percent of first-time students lived on campus (IUPUI Institutional Research and Decision Support 2017a). As the student population shifted to become more residential, new residence halls have been built to accommodate demand. There are now three residence halls and on-campus apartments. North Hall, the newest residence hall, completed in 2016, is the first traditional residence hall constructed at IUPUI since the campus was founded in 1969 (IUPUI Housing and Residential Life 2017b). Of the other two residence halls, Ball Residence Hall was built in 1928 and predates the founding of the university, and University Tower was formerly a university hotel, which was converted to a traditional residence hall in 2013 (IUPUI Housing and Residential Life 2017a). On campus, traditional residence halls feature dorm rooms with a dining hall in the facility, while other near-campus housing includes self-contained apartments. Off-campus housing options located within five miles of campus but not owned by the university have also grown (ForRentUniversity.com 2017).

University Library (UL), built in 1993, is the main campus library at IUPUI. Including UL, there are five campus libraries in total. The remaining libraries are the Ruth Lilly Law Library at the Law School, the Dental Library at the Indiana University School of Dentistry, the Art Library at the Herron School of Art, and finally the Ruth Lilly Medical Library on the medical campus. These other campus libraries primarily serve students in their respective programs. UL is the library for all other IUPUI students and students served by other campus libraries, since it is generally open more hours than the others. UL is centrally located on the IUPUI campus, and the other campus libraries are all about equidistant from UL. The research projects described here were conducted at UL and with students who would use UL, rather than other campus libraries.

MAPPING STUDY

In Fall 2015 IUPUI participated as one of eight universities in the "A Day in the Life" (ADITL) project, a multi-site ethnographic study of students' space use practices.[1] The study used a mixed-methods approach to data collection: combining text message (SMS) surveys delivered via students' cell phones and qualitative debrief interviews. The study examined space use by constructing a detailed map of each student's day, including tasks and activities, spaces and locations where the student did their work (both academic and day-to-day), and the ways the library and other campus locations fit within the student's overall educational experience. The use of mapping as a way to better understand the authentic student experience has been used frequently in library research (Cowan 2012; Delcore, Mullooly, and Scroggins 2009; Foster and Gibbons 2007; Khoo et al. 2013; Sharman 2017; Twiss-Brooks et al. 2017).

Methodology

The IUPUI Office of Institutional Research and Decision Support provided a sample of students from all majors and grade levels (except for the School of Medicine, which is technically an Indiana University Bloomington, rather than an IUPUI, program). Recruitment e-mails were sent to students and, from the initial list, $n = 31$ agreed to participate in the study. Of the original participants, $n = 27$ completed the text messages and debrief interview. Each was paid $20 for their participation in both the survey and the debrief. Participants chose one of two workweek days to receive the text message surveys. They were asked to choose a day of the week that would be most representative of their regular schedule. During the chosen day, each participant received 12 surveys about 75 minutes apart. Survey distribution was automated using the SMS functionality of Qualtrics, the online survey system. The 75-minute interval was chosen so that students would receive texts at different points of the hour, avoiding situations such as having every text arrive during a class period. The survey consisted of three questions: their location; what activity they were participating in; and how they felt at that time. Text message surveys started at 9:10 A.M. and ended at 10:55 P.M. Participants were instructed to wait to answer a text message if it would interrupt a class or be unsafe to answer (for example, while driving). In those cases, students were told to answer when it was feasible to do so and to indicate what they were doing when the original message arrived.

After the survey was completed, researchers used the responses to create a map for each student. The map was used to guide participants through a semi-structured debrief interview that sought to get more depth and nuance about their daily experiences, where and why they did their academic work, and other day-to-day activities. Each debrief interview took approximately one hour. During the debrief, exact locations (e.g., addresses) were elicited for each text event. These locations were entered into Google Maps to get exact latitude and longitude. This allowed for an analysis of the distance traveled and the distance between locations. Interviews were transcribed and coded using Dedoose qualitative data analysis software. The protocol was approved by the Indiana University Institutional Review Board (IRB).

Demographics

As previously stated, twenty-seven participants completed both the text message surveys and the debrief interview. Responses by student status were fairly equally distributed, with slightly lower participation from first-year and senior students. Note that no graduate students were recruited. This was deliberate, since graduate students typically have a much different academic and work schedule than undergraduate students. Only 22 percent of participants lived on campus, and 78 percent lived off campus.

A wide variety of majors were represented, with participants from each of the following: tourism and event management, psychology, mechanical engineering, communications, computer information technology, elementary education, nursing, sports management, biology, business, ceramics/French, dental hygiene, exercise science, geography and environmental science, media arts and science, respiratory therapy, and one undecided. The representation of majors is important, since other UL space use surveys have shown that students in majors whose buildings connect to the library (e.g., business, education) use the library more often. Significant for space planning, this study did a deep-dive into the location and study space preferences of many students whose departmental buildings are not next to UL.

SPACE STUDY

Prior to the renovation of the third and fourth floors of UL, library staff initiated a research plan to record the use of library spaces and evaluate student feedback on their use and students' perceptions of library spaces and services. The full plan included a space study, a library in-use survey, a survey of students who did not use the library, and data collected for public questions posted on whiteboards around the library. This chapter includes the results of the space study. Because the primary purpose of the study was to improve the service of the library and no identifying student information was recorded, it was deemed exempt by the Indiana University IRB.

The space study only included areas included in the renovation: the third and fourth floors of the library. The first floor of the library houses library administrative offices, technical services, the Center for Digital Scholarship, meeting rooms, and campus partnerships such as the Center for Teaching and Learning and the Office for the Vice Chancellor of Research. The second floor contains the circulation desk, a computer classroom, campus partnerships such as writing and math centers, and computer clusters. Because renovating them would require more costly structural work and negotiation with campus offices, and would not free up much space for additional student seating, it was deferred for a future renovation project. In contrast, the third and fourth floors are large, originally designed to house open stacks, and are easier to renovate. The third and fourth floors are similar in layout, with a mix of book stacks, computer clusters, and seating spaces, and there are few campus partners housed on those floors. Moreover, each floor also has a distinct environment that is controlled to foster different informal learning preferences. The third floor is a quiet floor, and contains seating arrangements intended for individual or paired study. The fourth floor is furnished with large tables and booth seating and is more conducive to group work and collaboration.

Methodology

Observation, when unobtrusive or passive, is a constructive way to collect data when use of a program, facility, or services is not directly connected to systems like a card reader or sign-in log (Biddix 2015). This method has long been a part of ethnographic research, and there is a recent increase in its use in library space assessment literature (Dominguez 2016; Hughes 2011; Linn 2013; Melssen 2014). A "seat sweep" is a method of observation in which the users in a defined area of the library are counted while a number of behavioral variables of those users are recorded (e.g., technology present, furniture in use, etc.) in timed intervals across a set number of days, weeks, or more. Analyzing library spaces to learn about students' preferred locations, most-used furniture types, and the activities students engage in can inform space-planning decision-making. As a result, library staff determined that this method would be useful in answering questions generated from the renovation research plan.

Working with campus architects and designers, library staff decided it would be most beneficial for the renovation design to observe a number of activities occurring on the third and fourth floors of the library during the peak period of the semester (during finals) and again during a period of more normal use of the building.[2] The observational intervals occurred every two hours beginning at 10:00 A.M. and ending at 6:00 P.M., a total of five observations per day, for five days, Monday-Friday. The first observation took place during the fifteenth week of the Fall 2016 semester, and the second observation occurred during the eighth week of the Spring 2017 semester. A team of approximately twenty library staff members volunteered to conduct the observation.

Library staff used Suma, an open-source, mobile, web-based assessment toolkit developed by North Carolina State University Libraries, to collect user counts. The Suma software platform, deployed on iPads, made it easy for staff to move quickly throughout library spaces and record data. The layout and interface were customized to develop a hierarchy named for specific areas on the third and fourth floors, and categories were added including group size, work surface type, and technology type. Inside each category was a list of attributes or activities. As library staff moved throughout the floors, they collected information within each area, choosing all the attributes and activities within each of the three categories that matched their observations.

A sample observation illustrates how this worked. An observer began by choosing the "East Window" area; as they moved through the area, they filled out each category. Two students sitting together (group size: "2") at a table (surface type: "table-small") appeared to be studying. The observer noted that one student had a textbook while the other was taking notes on a laptop. They both had snacks, and there were papers and notebooks across the table (technology: "book," "laptop," "food/drink," "printed documents"). Once all of the observations were recorded, the data was saved and stored on a secure library server.

Choosing to record predefined attributes and activities with Suma meant that observers sacrificed a certain degree of nuance because an open response box was not included in the data collection form. For this project, however, recording specific details about the activities and behaviors of library visitors was eschewed in favor of speed and quantity of data collection. By advertising that observation would take no more than one hour to complete, more library staff volunteered to observe and more observation times became possible. Training became easier as well, and saved researchers the need to decipher many separate shorthand note-taking techniques. Using the uniform Suma collection form was simple and straightforward to explain, and made it easy to add a significantly greater number of total observations to the dataset.

RESULTS

Mapping Study

The mapping study gave us a broad picture of how students spent their time.[3] Although not originally intended as a space study, this data has helped inform our space planning because it allows us to better understand students' use of space and their study space preferences. Most importantly, since the participant

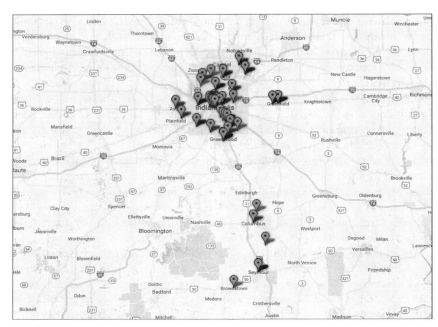

FIGURE 2.1

SMS study participant locations

sample was diverse, we captured data from library and non-library users. Not surprisingly, since a majority of participants commuted, students reported a lot of movement between campus, home, work, and other locations (figure 2.1).

However, although students had high ranges of distances traveled, this did not correlate to extensive commuting time (table 2.1). Parking was frequently mentioned as the worst thing about the campus and, betraying our roots as a commuter campus, lack of campus life was also mentioned as a negative. Overall, in survey responses, on a typical workweek day students reported spending the most time studying or doing other academic work (21 percent), with attending class (20 percent) and family, social, or recreational activities (19 percent) a close second and third. Respondents spent 12 percent of their time eating, 12 percent doing other things, 9 percent working, and 7 percent commuting.

TABLE 2.1

SMS study participant travel distances and times

MEDIAN DISTANCE TRAVELED (M)	MEDIAN REPORTED COMMUTE TIME (MIN)	MEDIAN ESTIMATED TIME (MIN)	AVERAGE DISTANCE BETWEEN LOCATIONS (M)
10,878	25	15	2,820

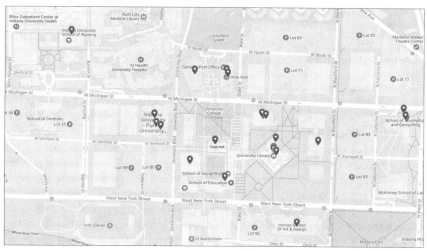

FIGURE 2.2
SMS study participant study locations on campus

When examining the campus locations in which students responded they were studying, classroom buildings, the University Library, and the campus center were the most frequent (figure 2.2; note that the campus center is indicated on the map with the large-print Indiana University-Purdue University). The qualitative debriefs gave us a more nuanced glimpse into student perceptions of the library, where students usually study, and why they preferred to study there. When students were asked about the day they participated in the surveys and why they studied where they did, convenience was a primary factor when choosing a study location. While they might not prefer to study at a certain location, if it fit into where they were coming from or going to, they would study anywhere. For example, "So I just stayed there [at the Nursing Building] and ate lunch and studied between the class and the test." Convenience also kept commuter students on campus for extended periods of time, rather than struggling with the overhead of parking. For example, one participant came to campus at 9:30 A.M. for a noon class, "so I sit around on campus for about two hours doing homework because I can't find parking." Residential students were more likely to pop in and out of study locations and go back to their dorm rooms.

When asked where they normally studied and why they liked studying there, many respondents indicated the library because it was quiet and the atmosphere facilitated studying.

> I like to study more [at the library] though, because I'm more focused than I am at home. I feel like at home all I want to do is lay in my bed. Every time I go home I just get into bed. But whenever I'm here I get everything done before I go home. So normally I'm on campus longer doing homework.

[Studying at the library] takes me out of my environment at home. My environment at home is way too comfortable. So it gets me upright at a desk. And I like it when other people are around but not in my business. So their vibes kind of keep me, keep me focused. And it's quiet.

As mentioned, the third floor of UL is designated as a quiet floor, and multiple respondents specifically mentioned the third floor as the place they preferred to study. Another large segment of respondents indicated they normally studied at their home because they liked being alone and all of their belongings are there. For example, "I just feel more comfortable at my house. And, I can wear whatever I want." While the overwhelming preference was for solo, quiet study space, a couple of respondents indicated they liked getting together with friends to study. Speaking to a continued need for computers, several respondents mentioned access to computers as a study space preference whether in the library or in computer labs across campus. Responses to a question asking about the difficulties of studying at IUPUI mirrored the previous question. Noise, finding study space or a computer, and finding plug-ins were frequently mentioned as difficulties.

Observation

Observation revealed several notable findings regarding student use of the library. The observed floors were busiest between 10:00 A.M. and 4:00 P.M., and each floor had unique occupancy patterns during these periods. The most notable trends in occupancy for both floors were the difference between Friday and the other weekdays, and the fact that more people chose to occupy seats on the fourth floor than the third (figure 2.3). A more detailed examination of the data, however, reveals several other differences between the two floors. The third, or quiet, floor saw greater variation between the times that observed library spaces were most and least occupied throughout the different periods of the day as well as throughout the week. The numbers recorded on Monday and Tuesday were significantly higher than those recorded during the rest of the week. In contrast, the collaborative fourth floor saw occupancy patterns that were much more consistent on a day-to-day basis, with usage following a similar pattern throughout the same periods of time each day. Additionally, the difference between the highest and lowest occupancy counts for the fourth floor was less extreme than the third floor; seating on the fourth floor was used more consistently throughout the hours of observation.

Most frequently, students were observed studying alone rather than in pairs or groups. Of $n = 10,076$, 86 percent of all students observed in the library were sitting alone, regardless of the floor. Students were observed studying in pairs 11 percent of the time, with groups of three to four students observed 3 percent of the time. Less than 0.5 percent studied in groups of five to six students and less than .05 percent of students were in groups of seven or more.

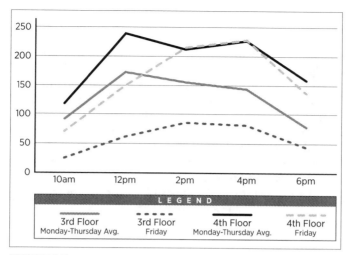

FIGURE 2.3

UL third- and fourth-floor usage patterns

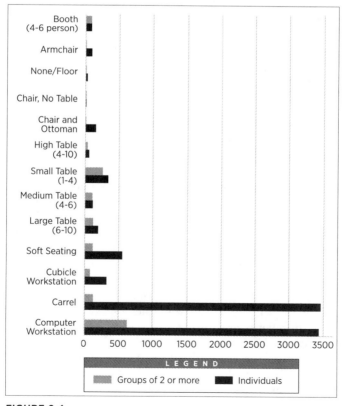

FIGURE 2.4

UL seating choices of individuals vs. groups

For those studying alone (n = 8,924), students overwhelmingly chose seating designed for or conducive to individual study such as carrels or computer workstations. However, in some cases individual students were observed using seating types that are most accommodating for groups of users, such as large tables, booth seating, or group cubicle workstations (figure 2.4). Looking proportionally, the seating choices for groups of two or more students (n = 1,623) mirrored the seating choices of individuals. In particular, groups of two or more students favored computer workstations. Groups chose to study together in carrels proportionally less than individuals, favoring computer workstations and tables of all sizes instead. Of the groups observed in carrels (n = 132), nearly all of them were groups of two.

INTERVENTIONS

The data collected in both the mapping and observational studies proved incredibly helpful to the design team working on the renovation. The findings allowed the group to set an agenda aimed at improving the quality of individual study on the third floor and the quality of collaborative study on the fourth floor. The campus administrators, architects, interior designers, and librarians working on the team all wanted to create spaces that improved the library experience for students. Though all parties did not initially agree on the best ways to accomplish this goal, the data collected by the studies helped the group to identify areas of opportunity.

Originally, campus administrators sought to create more group study space on both floors. However, by using student data that showed both the use and expressed value of the quiet floor, librarians were able to redirect the impulse to create new collaborative study space into improving noise quality and creating better study spaces for individuals and pairs. Students in the mapping study debrief mentioned the quiet floor in particular as an important place to study on campus. Observational data confirmed high usage of the area. Outside of this area, there is relatively little space designed for quiet study on the IUPUI campus. Data from these studies helped inspire designers to expand quiet study space by creating two silent rooms on the quiet floor. These rooms are enclosed in glass, and offer the added benefit of improving noise quality on the floor by deflecting noise upward through the library's atrium to the fourth floor. In addition, the observation revealed that many students on the quiet floor studied in pairs; yet the furniture in place did not easily facilitate this kind of study. Designers created seating on the third floor designed for two students to work side by side in a quiet environment.

The fourth floor was the library's most occupied floor during the periods of observation. The interior designers proposed removing computer workstations on this floor to create more space for collaboration, since many students have their own devices. Again, in this case, data from the studies changed the discussion. Many students in the mapping study indicated a preference for public computers, and 40 percent of students in the observational study were sitting at a computer workstation. It is possible that with a large population of commuter students, UL needs computers more than libraries on traditional campuses do. Commuter students may not always have technology with them as they travel between work, home, and class. Moreover, many students were observed using both library computers and personal devices, creating the effect of computing with multiple screens. With this information, the designers recommended keeping the existing computer workstations.

An area of the fourth floor renovated in 2013 to facilitate group study and collaboration was easily the most occupied portion of the library. Library staff encouraged the designers to increase collaborative study space on the fourth floor and, as a result, designers created space for open concept study rooms, partitioned with three walls and no doors. The library already has a cadre of forty-two reservable study rooms. The open concept study rooms are designed for serendipitous group study. Similar to some existing study rooms, these spaces will accommodate two to six students. Yet, these rooms differ from study rooms because they are constructed with only three walls, and students will be able to write on them with dry-erase markers. Furthermore, to address the observation results that demonstrate students' preference for sitting alone, the designers will also include a number of new modular seats and single-person study carrels.

CONCLUSIONS AND NEXT STEPS

IUPUI's history as a commuter campus has influenced faculty and staff to be both critical and industrious when it comes to applying best practices or embracing trends. Librarians, especially, understand that conventional practices that were studied and created in residential environments may not yield the intended results on an urban, mixed commuter and residential campus. As a result, research and assessment within the IUPUI context are often required before making significant campus changes.

UL has a strong and thriving culture of assessment. Librarians and library staff regularly engage assessment tools and reflection to ground the library's practice in evidence that is relevant to the unique experience of the IUPUI campus. Librarians frequently collaborate with each other to develop tools to offer insight into the interworking of library processes and service. UL administrators use data to guide the organization in the achievement of its mission and goals, and regularly encourage librarians to share the results of assessment projects.

The melding of these distinct studies has reinforced to librarians the importance of collaboration beyond library units. Strong inter-unit communication allowed these assessments to prove more powerful than if they had been analyzed and implemented separately. Both studies confirmed what library staff already suspected, that students prefer to study alone. This data gave librarians an advantage in articulating student needs in the design of new library space. Designers and campus administrators were receptive to developing spaces that accommodated students' existing study preferences, while also pushing innovative ideas into the designs.

The main limitation of the space study was its focus on the third and fourth floors of the library. This limit was imposed intentionally, because the campus administration chose to renovate only those floors of the building. However, this focus limits our ability to make generalizations about the patterns of movement and use of the whole library. This limitation is mitigated in part by the nature of public space at UL. The library is composed of five levels including a basement, of which public, student-facing library space is mainly on levels two, three, and four. Library staff effectively observed two-thirds of the public space. The limitations of the mapping study were similar to other studies with small sample sizes (for example, focus groups, usability testing) in that while there is greater opportunity to thoroughly understand the student experience, no statistically significant conclusions can be drawn from the dataset. There is also the issue of volunteer bias in that those who agreed to participate may have more interest in the library than those who didn't participate. There is no guarantee that the students who participated in the mapping study are representative of all IUPUI students.

Solo study space (e.g., carrels) and desktop computers may not be as in vogue as innovative collaborative spaces, but to ignore student preferences would be to not listen to our constituents, the primary users of the space. Additionally, the results of the mapping study raised questions of what (if anything) UL can do to help commuting students, especially since IUPUI has an almost equal mix of commuter (1,848) and residential (1,764) first-time, full-time beginner students (IUPUI Institutional Research and Decision Support 2017a). Though this number is on the rise and more off-campus options near campus are becoming available, the large majority of IUPUI students still qualify as commuter students. UL must recognize that circumstances beyond our control may influence space usage; for example, commuting students might sometimes view parking difficulties as a barrier to coming onto campus. We may do everything right and still not be able to reach some commuter students. Yet, for those students that do use the library, we will continue to work unceasingly to provide a twenty-first-century learning environment that is conducive to quiet study, active learning, collaboration, inspiration, and innovation. UL will adapt to meet the changing needs of our student population even as the campus transitions to its new, more residential identity.

REFERENCES

Biddix, J. Patrick. 2015. "Strategies for Assessing Commuter Students." *New Directions for Student Services* 150: 97–107. doi:10.1002/ss.20131.

Cowan, Susanna M. 2012. *Assessment 360: Mapping Undergraduates and the Library at the University of Connecticut.* Storrs, CT: University of Connecticut Libraries. https://www.clir.org/pubs/resources/Assessment360.pdf.

Dace, Karen, Anne L. Mitchell, Robbie Janik, Averie Hamilton, and the IUPUI Diversity Cabinet. 2016. *2016 IUPUI Diversity Report*. Indianapolis: Indiana University-Purdue University Indianapolis. https://diversity.iupui.edu/ Diversity_Report_2016_FINAL.pdf.

De Araujo, Pedro, and James Murray. 2010. "Estimating the Effects of Dormitory Living on Student Performance." Center for Applied Economics and Policy Research Working Paper #002–2010. Indianapolis: Indiana University-Purdue University Indianapolis. www.iub.edu/~caepr/RePEc/PDF/2010/ CAEPR2010–002.pdf.

Delcore, Henry D., James Mullooly, and Michael Scroggins. 2009. *The Library Study at Fresno State*. Fresno, CA: Institute of Public Anthropology, California State University. http://fresnostate.edu/socialsciences/anthropology/documents/ipa/ TheLibraryStudy(DelcoreMulloolyScroggins).pdf.

Dominguez, Gricel. 2016. "Beyond Gate Counts: Seating Studies and Observations to Assess Library Space Usage." *New Library World* 117 (5/6): 321–28. doi:10.1108/ NLW-08-2015-0058.

Evans, Tim. 2017. "Census Pushes Indianapolis Down One Spot to 15th Largest US City." *Indianapolis Star*. Retrieved from www.indystar.com/story/news/2017/ 05/25/three/345267001/.

ForRentUniversity.com. 2017. Indiana University-Purdue University-Indianapolis Off-Campus Housing. https://www.forrentuniversity.com/Indiana-University -Purdue-University-Indianapolis/+5-miles.

Foster, Nancy Fried, and Susan Gibbons, eds. 2007. *Studying Students: The Undergraduate Research Project at the University of Rochester*. Chicago: Association of College & Research Libraries.

Hughes, Annie M. 2011. "The Library as a Preferred Place for Studying: Observation of Students' Use of Physical Spaces." *Evidence Based Library & Information Practice* 6 (2): 61–63. doi:10.18438/B8VS6Q.

IUPUI. 2014. "Charles Bantz to Step Down as IUPUI Chancellor in August 2015." http://archive.news.iupui.edu/releases/2014/11/iupui-chancellor-charles-bantz -stepping-down.shtml.

———. 2017. "Strategic Initiatives." https://strategicplan.iupui.edu/Strategic Initiatives.

IUPUI Housing and Residence Life. 2017a. "First-Year Housing Options." http:// housing.iupui.edu/explore/first-year-housing/north/index.shtml.

———. 2017b. "History." http://housing.iupui.edu/about-housing/history.shtml.

IUPUI Institutional Research and Decision Support. 2017a. "Student Cohort Profiles and Outcomes. Lives in Campus Housing." IUPUI Data Link. http://irds.iupui .edu/Institutional-and-Strategic-Planning/IUPUI-Data-Link.

———. 2017b. "Student Enrollment." IUPUI Data Link. http://irds.iupui.edu/ Institutional-and-Strategic-Planning/IUPUI-Data-Link.

———. 2017c. "Student Enrollment by County, State, and Country." IUPUI Data Link. http://irds.iupui.edu/Institutional-and-Strategic-Planning/IUPUI-Data-Link.

Khoo, Michael, Lily Rozaklis, Catherine Hall, and Diana Kusunoki. 2013. "Identifying the 'Go-to Spots': Using Map Surveys to Elicit Perceptions of Space and Place in an Academic Library." *Proceedings of the Association for Information Science and Technology* 50 (1): 1–4. doi:10.1002/meet.14505001114.

Linn, Mott. 2013. "Seating Sweeps: An Innovative Research Method to Learn about How Our Patrons Use the Library." In *Imagine, Innovate, Inspire: Proceedings of the Association of College & Research Libraries Conference, 2013,* edited by Dawn M. Mueller, 511–17. Chicago: Association of College & Research Libraries. www.ala .org/acrl/conferences/acrl2017/papers.

Melssen, Maria. 2014. "Varying Student Behaviours Observed in the Library Prompt the Need for Further Research." *Evidence Based Library & Information Practice* 9 (1): 42–44. doi:10.18438/B8PK7G.

National Survey of Student Engagement. 2017. "The Relationship of Residence Life with Selected Engagement Measures." http://nsse.indiana.edu/html/sample_ analyses/relationship.cfm.

Sharman, Alison. 2017. "Using Ethnographic Research Techniques to Find Out the Story behind International Student Library Usage in the Library Impact Data Project." *Library Management* 38 (1): 2–10. doi:10.1108/LM-08–2016–0061.

Twiss-Brooks, Andrea B., Ricardo Andrade Jr., Michelle B. Bass, Barbara Kern, Jonna Peterson, and Debra A. Werner. 2017. "A Day in the Life of Third-Year Medical Students: Using an Ethnographic Method to Understand Information Seeking and Use." *Journal of the Medical Library Association* 105 (1): 12–19. doi:10.5195/ jmla.2017.95.

NOTES

1. The universities that participated in the full study were Indiana University Bloomington, Indiana University-Purdue University Indianapolis, Gustavus Adolphus College, University of Colorado Boulder, University of North Carolina Charlotte, NYC College of Technology CUNY, Borough of Manhattan Community College CUNY, and Brooklyn College CUNY. Protocols are available at the 2015 Library Assessment Conference proceedings, http:// libraryassessment.org/bm~doc/70-asher-2016.pdf.
2. Protocol is available at IUPUI ScholarWorks, "Suma Space Assessment Protocol," https://scholarworks.iupui.edu/handle/1805/13879.
3. For the SMS study, here we only report on the IUPUI part of that collaboration. Full eight-campus results were presented at the 2016 Library Assessment Conference, http://libraryassessment.org/bm~doc/70-asher -2016.pdf.

DONNA M. LANCLOS and
RACHAEL WINTERLING

3

Making Space in the Library for Student-Parents

I n February 2016, the University of North Carolina at Charlotte's Office of Adult Students and Evening Services (OASES) disseminated a report on the availability of courses and services for the university's adult students (Rogers 2016). The report made it clear that our campus has work to do to make its adult students feel well-served by the university. A bright spot was the students' relationship with and perception of the library, which was ranked in their survey as the second most valued service or department on campus. The J. Murrey Atkins Library saw this report as an opportunity to respond in a new way to the needs of our adult students.

INSTITUTIONAL CONTEXT

The University of North Carolina, Charlotte, or UNC Charlotte, is located in the suburbs of the city, near the upper arc of the freeway that encircles the greater Charlotte metro area. It is well-bricked and lushly landscaped, with botanical gardens on its western edge as well as parking lots ringing the entirety of the central campus. It is "North Carolina's Urban Research University," but its roots are as a two-year institution in the service of educating

GIs back from World War II; it became a four-year university in 1964 (Cone University Center 2017). In 2014/15 there were a total of 27,238 students enrolled, 5,002 (or almost 19 percent) of whom lived on campus (Office of Undergraduate Admissions 2017). Half of the new students who come to UNC Charlotte each year are transfer students from community colleges or other four-year universities—the "traditional" UNC Charlotte student, therefore, is nontraditional in many ways. The incoming class in 2014/15 was 35 percent "under-represented" students (African American, Asian, Hispanic, and other), and 65 percent white. An ongoing study of a day in the life of students, which includes UNC Charlotte students in the sample, highlighted commuting and parking as a central concern in how students organize their time and priorities around when and how they get to campus (Asher et al. 2017). Commuting to and from school and work—42 percent of our students work more than 20 hours per week while attending school—is a constant factor for the vast majority of the undergraduates, and for all of the graduate students at UNC Charlotte, none of the latter of whom live on campus. Students with children have additional layers of logistics to wrangle, in the equation of how and when to get to campus, as well as how and when they study anywhere at all.

The J. Murrey Atkins Library at UNC Charlotte is a centrally located ten-story building, and the primary library space on campus. In addition to four floors of space for study rooms and collections, there are four tower floors that contain collections and limited seating for patrons. Special Collections occupies the top two floors of the ten-story tower, with the reading rooms on the tenth floor open for all students. In addition to the open tables and chairs distributed throughout the library, particularly on the ground and first through third floors, students can reserve a variety of study spaces online, including group study rooms, individual study spaces, and gaming spaces. During the academic year, the library is open 24/5, and is open 24/7 during finals, although due to student demand, plans to experiment with 24/7 opening hours throughout the 2017/18 academic year were under discussion as of this writing. There is only one branch library at UNC Charlotte, in the architecture building.

THE ATKINS ETHNOGRAPHY PROJECT

Since 2009, the Atkins Ethnography Project has been directed by Donna Lanclos, who has conducted fieldwork and also coordinated and supervised ethnographic research by graduate students, undergraduates, and colleagues. The library ethnographer position at UNC Charlotte is equal parts researcher, program coordinator, and policy consultant, and has required engaging with a series of projects, large and small, to inform library policies around space, services, and digital environments (Lanclos 2016a; Lanclos 2015; Lanclos and Asher 2016; Kim Wu and Lanclos 2011). Ethics board renewal documents give us the number of consent forms we have collected over the lifetime thus far of the Atkins Ethnography Project, and as of 2016 we have collected consent forms from about 200 participants. We have also conducted observations and gathered information from groups in internal assessment exercises that do not require consent, so our total contact across the life of the project is greater than the numbers might indicate. Participants have been drawn from all academic colleges, all levels of educational status (undergraduate, graduate, and faculty), and from UNC Charlotte as well as University College, London (Gourlay, Lanclos, and Oliver 2015).

The larger research program of the Atkins Ethnography Project has been conducted via a series of self-contained but connected projects from 2010 through the present. The cumulative narrative of these projects and their outputs has delivered a much greater return for the library than each individual part, providing a larger context for each specific question we ask in any given investigation. In the Atkins Library, dedication to open-ended ethnography (emergent descriptive work generated by a long-term embedded presence) has coexisted with shorter projects that rely on a variety of instruments to elicit data, including observation, interviews, open forums and focus groups, mapping exercises, photo diaries, and easel/Post-It note quick feedback (Asher and Miller 2011; Foster and Gibbons 2007; Lanclos, Phipps, and White 2016; White and Le Cornu 2017).[1] None of these methods were separate from the work of the library, but were informed by and integrated into workflows. These methods were also not limited in their scope to the Atkins building, because of the role of the digital, and because teaching, learning, and research happen outside of the library. The results of the Atkins Ethnography Project are therefore relevant to academic places and practices throughout the university, and higher education generally.

THE FAMILY FRIENDLY LIBRARY ROOM

UNC Charlotte's Office of Adult Students and Evening Services (OASES) is charged with facilitating access to resources and information for our adult students. "Adult" has been in the past administratively defined as over the age of twenty-four, but that is no longer stated on the website (OASES 2017a), and there has long been a policy of allowing students to define themselves into the "adult student" category. One characteristic that makes students classify themselves as adults is if they have children, since the logistics of being a student and a parent at the same time can be a particular challenge.

The 2016 OASES report on the needs (met and unmet) of our adult students at UNC Charlotte's Atkins Library provided an opportunity for a partnership. We were particularly interested in hearing about the specifics of adult student needs, and the gaps between what they needed and what was available on campus. After some discussion, the Atkins Library and OASES partnered to establish a family-friendly study room in the library building, a "designated safe space for adult students and their children (ages zero to twelve) to thrive educationally" (OASES 2017b).

The ANSWER Family Friendly Library Room (FFLR; figures 3.1 and 3.2) was partly funded by a donor, via OASES, and partly funded by the library, and had its soft launch in July 2016. The library and the OASES office worked together to identify what furniture would be necessary to facilitate academic

Photo by Donna Lanclos

FIGURE 3.1
The ANSWER Family Friendly Library Room

Photo by Donna Lanclos

FIGURE 3.2
Soft seating and entertainment center, plus writable walls in the ANSWER Family Friendly Library Room

work, and what other items would make it possible for students to comfortably bring their children in while they study. The room is brightly painted, unlike the other study rooms in the library, and has one wall that has been made writable with whiteboard paint. There is soft seating for the children, a DVD player, and a computer for playing games.

From the time the room opened through March 2017 students acquired access to it by registering online at the OASES website. After approval, OASES sent their student card number to library facilities, which facilitated swipe access to the room. Students were told that the time between registration and card access to the room would be twenty-four hours, but that library security could let them into the room before swipe access was granted.

Methods

Because the Atkins Ethnography Project had been underway since 2010, we had the advantage of a series of studies that collectively yielded a wealth of information about the circumstances in which students traveled to campus: what their commute looked like, what they brought with them, where they had to be, and what obligations shaped when and how they were on campus.

For example, one of the photo items in the diaries is "all the stuff you take to campus," and we got photos of bags filled with books, paper notebooks, laptops,[2] pens, note cards and sticky notes, travel mugs, and phones and headphones. Another item was "your commute to campus" and we received many photos of cars, cars on freeways, and cars stopped at traffic lights. One student took a photo of the textbooks she needed for her classes, which she kept in a plastic milk crate in the trunk of her car, only carrying the ones she needed with her on relevant days.

The cognitive maps we collected from our undergraduate students who lived off campus were filled with motion, and places other than the university that they needed to be: work, home, and places such as cafes that were either better placed or better equipped (in terms of availability of food, drink, and opening hours) to serve their studying needs.

We came to the study of the FFLR, therefore, with a well-grounded sense of our student body at UNC Charlotte as having a large component of car-commuters, who had concerns about how much they have to bring to campus to study, and with obligations that extend beyond the university campus. Within this larger context, we approached the specific group of students who were our target audience for the FFLR: adult students.

We evaluated the use and impact of the FFLR in two ways. First, we used the statistics embedded in the Atkins Library room-booking software to get an overview of the time and frequency of the room's use.[3] Second, we recruited and interviewed students about their study habits, and how the FFLR did (or did not) fit into their academic practices.

Room Reservation Data

We have used the room reservation data as a proxy for occupation, since we did not have access to the swipe data for the rooms at the time of writing.

Statistics showed that the room was being reserved by a range of class levels, including graduate students. Largely absent are freshmen; most reservation records were made by seniors. The next most numerous bookings were made by master's degree students, then juniors, and then a sharp drop in the numbers of sophomores and PhD students.

We also found that there was a wide range of majors represented among students reserving the rooms, with students from each college on campus, including Engineering, Business, Liberal Arts and Sciences, Arts and Architecture, Education, Health and Human Services, and Computing and Informatics. This was significant because one of the concerns in providing this room was that it not serve a narrow range of students. It is clear that the needs of adult students cut across major courses of study, and are not limited to just one "kind" of student.

While most of the students booking the rooms were between the ages of 18 and 35, we also had older students using the room, including students in their mid to late forties, and also their fifties. Again, this helps us see that trying to predict whether someone would use this room based on age would not be especially useful; students of a wide range of ages needed this room to help them study.

We found the gender breakdown to be particularly interesting, as we compared the use of the FFLR with that of our study rooms in the library overall. The room-booking statistics revealed that female students booked study rooms in the library overall at a rate of nearly 20 percent higher than males, while female students booked the FFLR at twice the rate of male students. The currently reported gender breakdown on UNC Charlotte's campus is 51 percent male and 49 percent female (institutional statistics report gender as a binary, and use the terms "male" and "female"). This makes the fact that self-identified females book study rooms at a rate significantly more than males striking, and bears further investigation. It is true for both the FFLR and the general study room bookings, and so cannot be simply explained by the generalization that females are caregivers. We gather from other lines of evidence that the library is identified as a "safe" space on campus, and we are interested in further investigating this aspect of library occupation and motivations to be in the library.

We were also interested in the demand for the room over the course of the week, and whether it differed significantly from the overall patterns of study room bookings. Statistics revealed that Sunday, Monday, and Tuesday were the highest use days for the FFLR, and Friday was the lowest. The low Friday use rates could be because fewer classes are scheduled on Fridays, and student-parents tend to go to campus to study on days when they have classes.

The overall study room–booking patterns across the library are more active on Friday than the FFLR, and the FFLR is far more active on Saturday and Sunday than the general pattern, again highlighting the importance of weekends in the study lives of student-parents.

Qualitative Study Design and Methods

While the statistics gave us a sense of broad patterns of use of the FFLR as compared to other study rooms in the library, we needed qualitative research to reveal the practices and motivations of the students using the room. We designed this study to capture information before the occupation of the room and again after it had been used by students for an entire semester. We intended to conduct semi-structured pre-occupation interviews in the summer before the room officially opened at the beginning of the Fall semester, and then to conduct post-occupation interviews, ideally with some of the same students, in the beginning of the Spring semester.

Before the FFLR opened, we worked to identify and interview some of the students who intended to use the room. OASES had publicized the room, and students had already signed up to be eligible for swipe access; we e-mailed those students to recruit them for the interviews. Our intention with these

TABLE 3.1

FFLR student demographics

FFLR	AGE	ETHNICITY	GENDER	YEAR AT UNCC	TRANSFER?	G/UG	FULL OR PART TIME?	MAJOR	AGES OF CHILDREN
1	31	white	F	3 (junior)	N	U/G	FT	English	8, 9, 11
2	41	white	F	senior	Y	U/G	FT	Psych	8, 12, 10.5
3	25	white	F	senior	Y	U/G	FT	Biology, Chem minor	4 (5 in July)
4	36	Asian	M	1st year	N	Grad	FT	Data Science and Business Analytics	4.5
5	27	white	F	3 (senior)	Y	U/G	FT	Economics	7, 5, 17 months, newborn
6	38	black	F	3 (senior)	Y	U/G	PT	Sociology and Women and Gender Studies	20, 13
7	24	white	F	2nd year	N	Grad	FT	English	3
8	25	white	F	senior	Y	U/G	PT	English	5

interviews was to capture the expectations and hopes that our students had for the new FFLR. We conducted five pre-occupation interviews in all for this part of the assessment, two by phone, and three face-to-face. We conducted all of the post-occupancy interviews face-to-face, except for one conducted by phone. Altogether, we interviewed eight students for this project (table 3.1), and two of these students we interviewed twice, once before the room opened and once after.

FINDINGS

Pre-Occupation Themes

Our content analysis of the pre-occupation interview transcripts revealed two primary themes for the student-parents we interviewed, both centering on distraction. There were also some specific requests from the students we interviewed about the FFLR.

Being Distracted

Students who have had no choice but to study at home with their children talked about the difficulties of being at home. One student said, "I like to be on campus, it gives me a focused mindset, with less distraction. I tried bringing my son in [to Atkins Library], it was distracting for me, distracting for other people." The students were easily distracted by family and other obligations at home, found it hard to focus, and may not have had a designated space for studying. To cope with these difficulties, students talked about studying when their children are sleeping, or are busy with other activities such as school or recreational activities. They also tended to schedule classes around their children's schedule, resulting in restricted times that they could be on campus, even if studying at home was less than optimal.

Being a Distraction

Students were worried about their children being loud and bothering other students, and that worry was distracting. One student felt self-conscious having a child with her, and expressed a fear of being judged. A dedicated family-friendly study room was interpreted by one student as evidence that they as student-parents are respected, acknowledged, and wanted on campus. The room was seen as something that can help set expectations for studying for students themselves and their children. One student expected that the room would allow him to use the library more than he had been doing, because he could "spend more time without disturbing others." Another student stated that she had never tried to study with her children in the library, because she just assumed they would be too loud.

Specific Desires for the Room or Services

Students wanted the FFLR to have the following characteristics and qualities:

- Somewhere they can find focus
- Comfortable and quiet
- Contains something for children to do, and comfortable furniture for them to sit on
- Available for group study
- Well-marketed and advertised
- Enclosed and separated from the general library space
- Facilitates study with fellow majors
- Separation between self and child within a contained study room

In feedback unrelated to the FFLR, we had learned of a desire for lockers in the library (or elsewhere on campus) to leave belongings there instead of having to carry them all over campus. Students in this study and in other studies of the Atkins Ethnography Project frequently discussed the sheer amount of "stuff" they brought with them to campus. For example, one student in this study always brought a laptop, and kept her backpack with all of her books in her car, so that she could access what she needed throughout the day. Another student described all of the things she took to campus with her, including food, and the size of the bag she needed to bring to fit it all in. She kept some of her supplies in her car, and at lunch switched out things she needed for the afternoon. The desire for lockers by commuter students, in this context, makes sense.

Students were aware that time spent commuting had an impact on when they went to campus, and how much time they spent there, how much time they had for studying, and all of the other things they had to do as students and parents. One student scheduled morning and evening classes on some days so that she could stay on campus the entire day, to fit in a week's worth of studying in that time. Concern about the time taken to commute to campus and to other places students needed to be was also reflected in concerns collected from prior interview data (Asher et al. 2017). Most UNC Charlotte students have to deal with commuting and parking, which are significant sources of logistical and financial stress, even without the additional consideration of parenting logistics. There are additional implications for students who are parents, who also have to factor in time for caregiving, transporting children to and from school and day care, and the fact that they do not always have a chance to study at home, because of the needs of their families as well as the requirements they have for effective study environments.

Overall, the pre-occupation feedback from the students we interviewed was positive. Particularly striking were student statements such as: "Just knowing there is a group of people who cares is amazing." Another student expressed excitement about the room, noting that she felt student-parents are a "forgotten population." The affective impact of library services which indicate that we know and are paying attention to the specific needs of our students, and that we care, cannot be underestimated. Providing "just" one room for student-parents might seem like a small gesture, but to the students we interviewed, the room and what it represented were clearly significant.

POST-OCCUPATION THEMES

Additional themes emerged from our analysis of the interviews we conducted after the students had used the rooms, including access, planning, surprise, technical difficulties, focus, inclusivity, modeling university, and commuting and parking.

Access

Technical difficulties with the swipe (and lack of local control) meant that some students could not get into the room in enough time for it to be useful. This made them less likely to try to use the room, or meant that when they did use it, they did not have as much study time as they would have if their swipe had worked. One student had the experience of her swipe card not working, but her study group members' (none of whom were registered to use the room) cards did. One student, on the day she used the room, kept packing up all of her things and bringing them with her to bring her potty-training child to the bathroom, because she had to leave the door open so she could get back into the room, and was unsure about security. Of note is that generally the online booking of the room was perceived to be easy.

Planned vs. Spontaneous Use

Patterns of use varied: some students planned their use of the room around their children's school schedules and reserved the room accordingly. Other students learned at the last minute, often because of plans falling through, that they would need to bring their child to campus, and dropped in on the room to use it. One student was told about the FFLR at the circulation desk as she stood there with her child, and otherwise would not have known about the room or used it that day. Another only needed to use it when doing group work, and so knew ahead of time to book it. One graduate student used it when his children were out of school on days he needed to go to the university to study.

Surprise

Student-parents expressed pleased surprise that there was a range of things for their children to do, while they themselves were studying. Their expectations had been fairly low—books, a place to sit perhaps—and the DVD player, writable wall, and other furniture options made them very happy. One student enjoyed the decorations on the walls so much she Snapchatted about it with her friends. Another student expressed surprise at how quiet the room was, especially at night, when she assumed students would be "more relaxed (and noisy)," and also about how nice the equipment was in the room—she assumed it would be "bum" computers, not the new machines with fast Internet that were provided.

Technical Difficulties

Aside from getting into the room, some students could not figure out how to get the DVD player and other equipment to work, and they lost study time trying to figure these out before giving up. One student's young daughter was expecting touch-screen capabilities on the laptop, which meant she did not know how to use the technology without her mother's help; the provided headphones also did not fit this child, who was younger than the intended age for the headphone set we provided. The time she spent trying to figure out the technology was time that this student did not have to study.

Focus

The room gave students a space where they knew they could study, which saved them the time they might otherwise have spent trying to find a spot that would accommodate their children and not distract either the student-parent or any other students. One student said she valued the "quiet space away from other students." Another noted that when she studied at home, it took her much longer, because the opportunities to be distracted were so numerous. And a third student noted that while she had Internet and computers at home, the "educational environment" of the library made it easier for her to study and be focused: "There's only so much you can do in this room," she said. "Having that space to be alone with my thoughts was crucial."

Modeling University

One of our interviewees valued bringing her tween to study with her on campus, so her child would see the university as a destination, and as a possibility, far sooner than she herself had. She felt it made her "daughter feel like she's in college." Being in the library was a good atmosphere for them both, and confirmed what she had been telling her daughter about college and what college was going to look like. Though this was not one of the intentions of the room, it is interesting that this was one of the impacts. As with the pre-occupation feelings of care that the room engendered, this impact is about how the student feels; such emotional impacts are an important part of the overall effect of library policies and decisions.

Inclusivity

One student made a point of mentioning how nice it was that the room demonstrated that the university "sees" students who are also parents: "It's small, but it's a shout-out to 'we see you' on campus." She interpreted the presence of the room and the thought that was put into fitting it out with entertainment options for the children as evidence that the university cares about student-parents. Another student noted that the room was useful for her to study with group members, none of whom had children. In this case, the room is not only an effective demonstration of the university's care for this category of nontraditional student, but also a chance for students who are not parents to witness their nontraditional peers and expand the notion of what "being a student" might be.

Commuting and Parking

All of the students we interviewed drove to campus and paid to park. None of the parking lots are close to the library. The challenges of commuting were made particularly clear in the story of one student who had a parking pass during the first summer this room was open. She used the room often during the Summer session, sometimes bringing her child with her and sometimes alone. In the Fall semester, she could no longer afford the parking pass; instead, she parked near her daughter's school and took the bus the rest of the way to campus. She noticed a difference in how prepared for her classes she felt in the fall compared to the summer, and attributed it to the hour of studying that she used to have when she parked on campus, rather than on the bus where she found it impossible to study. It has "definitely hindered my progress [to degree]," she said. This student worked four jobs to make ends meet. This student spoke a great deal about her catch-22 situation: she needs the time to study, to get better grades and scholarships, but she needs the jobs she is working to pay for her classes. She is studying part-time now because "I can only afford two [courses], mentally and financially."

Another student noted that her commute was easy precisely because of when her classes are—she is a graduate student, so coming to campus at night means parking is relatively easy, and traffic is light.

LEARNING FROM NON-USERS

Of interest is the one student we interviewed from the pre-occupation who ended up not using the room at all in the Fall semester. This student, as a biology and chemistry major, had access to a lab and project space in the building that houses her academic departments, and so she did not need to use the FFLR. The spaces she had worked for her because they were close to where she needed to attend classes, and to the people with whom she needed to work on projects. The lab and project space contained people who already knew her, and her child, and who would tell her (kindly) if the child was being a bother.

She said of the lab space she had access to, "It's quiet, I know the people in there, and I can find a seat," in contrast to the library, where in her experience she had to look for places to sit, and to worry about being more quiet. She mentioned that one time during the previous semester, she had come into the library to try to study, on the spur of the moment. It was at the end of the semester, and the library was so crowded that she left immediately. She was not willing to go into any of the study rooms and risk getting kicked out by someone who had a reservation.

This student also wished that the kinds of spaces available to her were also available in the building where she took her biology classes. She thought having study rooms in each building, closer to where people have their own majors, would be better than always having to go "out of the way to get to a crowded library." At the same time, she said she would like to see spaces like that across campus; she wondered if there were some that she did not know about because she spent all her time in one particular building.

PROBLEM-SOLVING AND NEXT STEPS

Technical barriers around access and use of the technology have a direct impact on how much time students have to study, and if they have to spend time overcoming barriers, they have less time for their academic work. Once the room was opened, the primary barrier to use was access to the room via the swipe system. The fact that access was not automatic upon registration prevented some students from using the room right away. The library has corrected this with programming by the team in Atkins Digital Initiatives. Additional specific fixes to address problems that students encountered have been implemented. Basic instructions for the recreational technology are now posted in the room. Additionally, more than one size of headphones and speakers are now available so that children of a wider range of ages can use the DVD player and other devices that require audio output.

The room-booking data indicates a wide range of ages, majors, and class levels, and it indicates that mothers as well as fathers are using the FFLR. This allows us to argue that this room is relevant to many of our students, opens doors across the university, and is certainly not being used by any narrow group (however it might be defined) alone. The overall pattern of FFLR use across the semester is very similar to that of library rooms overall, but use across the week is distinctive, with more parents relying on weekend hours than the statistics reflect for the general study room bookings.

Our biggest recommendation is that this room be far more widely publicized. The need for spaces such as this on campus for our student-parents is clearly great, and as many students as possible should know that this is available for them to use. It would be a good "problem" for us not to have enough capacity with just one room, and to have to make the argument for larger, or additional, such spaces.

We will continue to monitor use of the rooms using the proxy of the booking software, and we plan to work with the OASES office to gather feedback on what is working, and what is not, in the current room. We are waiting for another round of renovations of our second floor, where the FFLR is currently located, before experimenting with possibly adding another FFLR. One FFLR could be for students needing to work alone, as the current room is configured, and another could be for students who need to work with study groups. The group study FFLR could be furnished with a large central table, several task chairs, and writable walls not just for the children to write on, but for the students to do their academic work.

CONCLUSIONS

The pre-occupation phase of this study uncovered an enthusiasm among adult students for the idea of a Family Friendly Library Room, as well as the reasons why such a room is desired and necessary for some of our students who are parents. Parents who could not always study at home, who sometimes needed to bring their children to campus but who worried about disturbing others, and who wanted a comfortable place to do their academic work (both quiet and focused, and not), saw the potential usefulness of this new library study space. Students were furthermore heartened by what they saw as evidence of the university's care for them, and their particular circumstances as parents.

Our student-parents are operating in a larger context than just the university, and what the library does or does not provide is not the entire picture of their needs. We heard anxiety from students about commuting and parking, and the time and money they spend on these activities, and the real impact it has on their studies and academic engagement. We plan to share these issues with the larger university community, since this is not something that can be addressed or mitigated by the library alone.

In addition, the student we interviewed who never used the FFLR did not use it in part because she had access to effective learning spaces on campus that suited her informal learning needs, in a community she knew and trusted. Her sense that there is a wider network of student-centered spaces across campus is reflected in our collection of cognitive maps of student learning landscapes, which reveal that students need to study in spaces across the university, not just in classrooms or in the library (Lanclos 2016b; Gourlay, Lanclos, and Oliver 2015). Our continuing attempts to imagine, fund, and produce a distributed landscape of informal learning spaces that we have been calling "Atkins Spaces" is one solution to the continuing desire of students for places to do their academic work close to the other places where they need to be. How can the library help provide more of those places?

When libraries engage in qualitative space studies, questions about impact reach beyond library walls. Engaging in holistic approaches to students' study practices and needs, such as we have done here, de-centers the library and allows us to imagine contexts that meet students where they are, where they have to be because of the complicated circumstances of their lives. In so doing, we make university experiences more accessible to a wider range of people, by not insisting that their status as parents put undue limits on how and where they study, and ultimately their success as students.

REFERENCES

Asher, Andrew, Juliann Couture, Jean Amaral, Maura Smale, Barbara Fister, Donna Lanclos, Sara Lowe, and Mariana Regalado. 2017. "A Day in the Life: Practical Strategies for Understanding Student Space-Use Practices." In *Proceedings of the 2016 Library Assessment Conference: Building Effective, Sustainable, Practical Assessment, October 31–November 2, 2016, Arlington, VA*, edited by Sue Baughman, Steve Hiller, Katie Monroe, and Angela Pappalardo, 428–38. Washington, DC: Association of Research Libraries. http://libraryassessment .org/archive/conference-proceedings-2016.shtml.

Asher, Andrew, and Susan Miller. 2011. "So You Want to Do Anthropology in Your Library? A Practical Guide to Ethnographic Research in Academic Libraries." ERIAL Project. www.erialproject.org/wp-content/uploads/2011/03/Toolkit -3.22.11.pdf.

Cone University Center, UNC Charlotte. 2017. "About Bonnie E. Cone." https://cone .uncc.edu/about-bonnie-e-cone.

Foster, Nancy Fried, and Susan L. Gibbons, eds. 2007. *Studying Students: The Undergraduate Research Project at the University of Rochester*. Chicago: Association of College & Research Libraries.

Gourlay, Lesley, Donna M. Lanclos, and Martin Oliver. 2015. "Sociomaterial Texts, Spaces and Devices: Questioning 'Digital Dualism' in Library and Study Practices." *Higher Education Quarterly* 69 (3): 263–78. doi:10.1111/hequ.1207.

Kim Wu, Somaly, and Donna Lanclos. 2011. "Re-Imagining the Users' Experience: An Ethnographic Approach to Web Usability and Space Design." *Reference Services Review* 39 (3): 369–89. doi:10.1108/00907321111161386.

Lanclos, Donna M. 2016a. "Embracing an Ethnographic Agenda." In *User Experience in Libraries: Applying Ethnography and Human-Centred Design,* edited by Andy Priestner and Matt Borg, 21–37. New York: Routledge.

———. 2016b. "Ethnographic Approaches To the Practices of Scholarly Communication: Tackling the Mess of Academia." *Insights* 29 (3): 239-48.

———. 2015. "Case Study 4.2, Ethnographic Techniques and New Visions for Libraries; Going beyond the numbers: using qualitative research to transform the library user experience." In *Library Analytics and Metrics: Using Data to Drive Decisions and Services,* edited by Ben Showers, 96–107. London: Facet Publishing.

Lanclos, Donna, and Asher, Andrew D. 2016. "'Ethnographish': The State of the Ethnography in Libraries." *Weave: Journal of Library User Experience* 1 (5).

Lanclos, Donna M., Lawrie Phipps, and David White. 2016. "Visitors and Residents, Mapping Your Digital Engagement." https://drive.google.com/drive/u/0/folders/0B_sfm89i9DC9azJwTk9WQmdwMDg.

OASES Office of Adult Students and Evening Services, UNC Charlotte. 2017a. "About Us."

———. 2017b. "ANSWER Scholarship Family-Friendly Library Room in Atkins Library." http://oases.uncc.edu/programs/answer-scholarship-family-friendly-library-room-atkins-library.

Office of Undergraduate Admissions, UNC Charlotte. 2017. "University Profile." https://admissions.uncc.edu/about-unc-charlotte/university-profile.

Rogers, Kimberly. 2016. "Review of Course Availability and Services for Adult Students at UNC Charlotte." Unpublished white paper, Office of Adult Students and Evening Services, UNC Charlotte.

White, David, and Alison Le Cornu. 2017. "Using 'Visitors and Residents' to Visualise Digital Practices." *First Monday* 22 (8). http://firstmonday.org/ojs/index.php/fm/article/view/7802.

APPENDIX

Research Methods

Recruitment

Because the sign-up for the ANSWER Family Friendly Study Room is online, the Atkins Library has access to the list of log-ins for the students currently signed up. We used that list to e-mail students asking if they were interested in speaking to us about what they might be expecting from the room. We did not offer any incentives. At the very beginning of the summer of 2015 (June), we had five volunteers for the pre-occupation interviews.

To recruit for the post-occupation second phase, we e-mailed students, using the contact list we generated from the room-booking software, which gave us the e-mail addresses of students who had reserved the room during the Summer or Fall terms. The OASES office also sent out a call for volunteers, and we followed up with students who had spoken to us before the room opened. Altogether, we interviewed eight students for this project, and two of these students we interviewed twice (once before the room opened, and once afterwards).

Interview Questions and Protocols

This project was reviewed by UNC Charlotte's Institutional Research Board and covered by the ethics protocol on file for the Atkins Ethnography Project at UNC Charlotte.

The pre-occupancy structured interview questions were:

1. Tell me about where you have been studying. What kinds of places work for you?

2. Do you study in different places for different kinds of work? Tell me about those places

3. Where do you live? How long is your commute?

4. How long do you usually study for? Does it look different for different kinds of work?

5. What is not working in the places you study now?

6. Why do you want to use the Family Friendly Study Room?

7. What are you hoping the Family Friendly Study Room will be like?

8. Do you already know about any resources or materials in the library that would be useful to you while you are here with your kids?

Each interview took between 20 and 45 minutes. Interviews were audio-recorded, and we also took notes during the interviews. Only one interview was conducted face-to-face, in the pre-occupancy phase; all of the rest were conducted by phone. Once the interviews were transcribed, we read and coded them, engaging in content analysis to identify themes emerging from the interviews as a whole.

Post-occupancy interview questions included:

1. Have you used the FFLR at all?

2. Why did you use it?

3. What worked?

4. What would you like to be different?

5. What expectations did you have that were met?

6. What was unexpected?

7. What do you wish it had been like?

8. Would you use the room again?

These interviews also took between 20 and 45 minutes. All but one of the post-occupancy interviews were conducted face-to-face. This time, the interviews were not transcribed, but the detailed notes taken during the interviews were coded, identifying themes in common with the previous set of interviews as well as new themes.

Recruiting Script

The e-mail text read as follows:

"Hello there—

I am Donna Lanclos, and I work for Atkins Library as an anthropologist. That means I talk to students and faculty about what they do for their classes and their research, and in particular about what works and what doesn't work for them. The idea is to get the right kind of information so we can improve our spaces, services, and so your experience and education at UNC Charlotte.

I have your name as one of the students signed up to use our new family friendly study room in the Fall, and would love to be able to talk to you (f2f, over phone, or Skype) about your hopes and expectations for that room, as well as about how and where you have been studying up until now.

Of course, this is not mandatory, and you can say no. If you are willing to talk to me, it shouldn't take more than 45 minutes to an hour tops. Also, if we talk over the summer, I would like to have a follow-up conversation or two in the Fall and/or Spring, to check in on how things are going.

So, if you are interested, please e-mail me back and let me know. And thank you so much."

NOTES

1. For a nice overview of a possible range of methods used in ethnographic research in academic libraries, see Asher and Miller 2011.
2. Many students have laptops but leave them at home because of concerns over battery life and being able to find a place to charge them, loss or theft, and not wanting to carry them around all day.
3. Thanks are due to Derek Norton in the Atkins Library's Digital Initiatives Department for helping us export the statistics from the software.

4

Beyond the Bubble

Undergraduates, Commuting, and the Academic
Library at a Flagship Public University

S tudents at flagship public universities often fit the profile of a traditional undergraduate student in the United States. They enter college after high school, are generally between the ages of 18 and 24, are dependents, work part-time or not at all, and are enrolled as full-time students. While there have been explorations of the academic library situated within students' lived experiences in different campus settings, there has been little examination of the role of student commutes (Duke and Asher 2012; Foster and Gibbons 2007). The studies that have examined students' commutes are situated on campuses that identify as commuter schools (Regalado and Smale 2015; Delcore, Mullooly, and Scroggins 2009; Brown-Sica 2012). Large public universities, where it is often assumed that students' lives are centered on or adjacent to campus, are largely unexamined.

At the University of Colorado Boulder (CU Boulder), the main campus and the surrounding area are often referred to as "the bubble," suggesting that students' lives are primarily contained in this area. The university is faced with the related challenges of accommodating increased enrollment on a campus with limited growth opportunities, identifying parts of town where the campus can expand, and being situated in an area with a rising cost of living, especially related to housing costs. As the university tackles these issues, what impact do these same challenges have on students' academic lives and where they live, work, and study? Currently, very little is known about how CU Boulder students travel to and within campus spaces and the barriers they face.

At CU Boulder, researchers in the library studied a typical academic day for undergraduate students as part of a larger, multi-institutional project comparing undergraduate experiences across the United States. This study revealed that the commutes of CU Boulder undergraduate students were more complex than anticipated, including those who lived in on-campus housing. In examining our students' daily lives, we found that many factors influenced where students live and how location impacted their commutes and academic work. Moving to off-campus housing often allowed for a less complicated commute and provided the individual student with greater control over her study environment. A deeper understanding of how our students moved between home, class location, workplaces, extracurricular activities, and other commitments illuminates gaps in library services, spaces, and resources and helps identify possible partnerships with other campus initiatives.

INSTITUTIONAL CONTEXT

CU Boulder is a flagship, public university with 33,771 students, 27,846 of whom are undergraduates. The university is a national public research university that provides a rigorous education, supports the community, and ensures access. The average age for a CU Boulder undergraduate student is 20.4 years of age, with only 5 percent of undergraduate students over the age of 25 (University of Colorado Boulder 2017a). A majority of our undergraduate student population can be categorized as traditional college students: they are dependents and are not responsible for caring for any other family members. As a state institution, a majority of our undergraduate student body, approximately 60 percent, is comprised of Colorado residents, and 7 percent of undergraduates are international students. Almost 70 percent of the undergraduate student body identifies as white, non-Hispanic, while 2 percent identify as black or African American, 5 percent as Asian, 11 percent as Hispanic/Latino, and 5 percent as two or more races. In the 2016/17 academic year, 1,133 undergraduate transfer students enrolled in CU Boulder (University of Colorado Boulder 2017a). Based on academic year 2016/17 financial aid data, approximately 17 percent of students were dependents that were Pell Grant eligible, while 54 percent either demonstrated no financial need or did not submit a FAFSA.

The CU Boulder campus is situated in the southern part of Boulder, a city with a population of roughly 100,000 people. The main portion of campus is over 300 acres and contains academic buildings, student support services, and thirteen residence halls. On the southern edge of campus is a section known as the Kitteridge loop that contains a planetarium, the law school, and a cluster of six residence halls. Approximately a mile and a half from the center of campus is Williams Village (Will Vill), a 66-acre residential academic village containing five residence halls, a dining facility, and more recently, student support services such as tutoring and health services. This area is connected to the main campus by a multi-use path and a university shuttle bus known as Buff Bus that runs every twenty minutes. East Campus was recently developed on an additional 200 acres located approximately a mile away from the main portion of the university, and is comprised primarily of research centers and institutes. As university enrollment and programs continue to expand, other areas of town, particularly another 300 acres on the southern edge of Boulder, are being identified and developed for campus expansion to provide additional residence halls, academic buildings, and research facilities.

First-year students at CU Boulder are required to live on campus unless they obtain a waiver for alternative housing arrangements, such as living at home or with other relatives, resulting in approximately 95 percent of first-year students living on campus. While CU Boulder is not known as a commuter campus, in fact only 26 percent of its undergraduate students live in campus-owned and operated housing, leaving only 1,100 students residing on campus after their first year (University of Colorado Boulder 2017a). While there is no official tracking of off-campus housing, CU Boulder's Office of Institutional Data estimates that based on the provided home addresses of students, approximately 4,000 students reside in areas outside of Boulder zip codes (University of Colorado Boulder 2017b). Available data suggests that these students commute anywhere from 20 to 90 minutes from their home location to campus. There is little information available regarding CU Boulder students' selection of off-campus housing, but housing affordability is a concern in Boulder due to its limited and costly rental market. Students comprise approximately 14 percent of the Boulder rental market, where the average monthly rent is now $1,418 (U.S. Department of Housing and Urban Development 2017). Increased enrollments have resulted in on-campus housing reaching capacity, and the university is currently in the process of building another residence hall to accommodate an additional 575 students.

The CU Boulder University Libraries is comprised of five library locations situated in areas throughout the main portion of campus. Norlin Library is often referred to as the main library and is a large, sprawling building at the base of a main quad. It has seen numerous additions throughout the years, which have resulted in five floors and complex navigation. In addition to housing various book stack locations, library instruction spaces, a learning commons, and common library functions, Norlin Library also includes an outpost of the Writing Center, IT support, the Honors Program, and other university programs. There are four branch library locations situated in academic buildings: Business, Earth Sciences, Music, and Math, Physics, and Engineering. The University Libraries is currently running a pilot program to provide access to library materials to researchers located on the East Campus, but it has yet to expand services and resources aimed at undergraduates much beyond the central portion of campus. A recent examination of campus space use determined that the University Libraries had insufficient space for student use. Our Association of Research Libraries peers on average have seating capacity to accommodate 10.5 percent of FTE students, whereas CU Boulder can accommodate only 6.8 percent of FTEs across all five library locations (Huron Education 2015). This assessment of space has provided a push to increase the libraries' seating capacity for student use, and different locations are considering how to reimagine spaces in such a way to increase the number of available seats while maintaining the connection to library services and resources.

A DAY IN THE LIFE

The "A Day in the Life" project sought to holistically understand the lives of undergraduate students across the United States, with CU Boulder one of eight participating institutions. Student research participants indicated one of two weekdays to receive a series of text message surveys. These messages were sent seventy-five minutes apart and asked the students to share their current location, indicate the activity they were engaging in, and how they felt at the time. After the survey was completed, the research team created a map of each student's day that was used to guide an interview about the student's daily tasks and activities, the spaces and locations in which the student conducted academic research and day-to-day work, and the student's overall educational experience. Students were asked to describe other life factors such as employment, extracurricular activities, and decisions around university selection, in addition to academic work and study habits. All study protocols were approved by the Institutional Research Board (Asher et al. 2017).

Participants at CU Boulder were recruited through flyers and handouts in five library locations across campus and through a posting on an electronic bulletin site that announces research studies and other campus events. These various recruitment efforts were used to capture students who regularly used the libraries, along with those who relied on other locations for academic work. This led to a convenience sample of 25 participants, 20 of whom were undergraduate students who completed the day's responses and the follow-up interview. All participants were full-time undergraduate students covering a range of academic years and majors, 6 were transfer students, and 15 indicated working part-time, with hours worked ranging from 5 to 30 per week. Of those that worked, most had employment off campus or had a mixture of on-campus and off-campus employment. Sixteen students identified as white, two as Hispanic/Latino, one as African American, and one as Asian. A majority of students resided in off-campus housing, with only four students living in residence halls, all of whom were first-year students.

UNDERSTANDING STUDENTS' DAILY LIVES AND COMMUTING BEHAVIORS

Survey responses allowed us to map each student's daily movements and determine distance between points throughout the day. These stops included home, work, class locations, study spots, and recreational and social activities. While the geocoded data centered around the campus, the debriefing interviews demonstrated that students' daily movements are far more complex by highlighting gaps in student maps and variations based on the day of the week.

Distances Traveled and Time Spent on Activities

Based on survey responses, CU Boulder participants traveled a median distance of 8,001 meters, with a median reported commute time of ten minutes and an average distance between locations of 1,557 meters. Students distributed their time in a single academic day similarly to those at other institutions across the United States, spending 27.6 percent of their time studying, 19.3 percent spent in class, and 7.3 percent of their time commuting (Asher et al. 2017). On a typical academic day, most students' map points were

FIGURE 4.1

Student home locations within the city of Boulder, CO

between home, class, and studying or other academic work. Points identified as off-campus employment often fell later in the day, while work at on-campus jobs commonly occurred before or between classes. Compared to other primarily residential institutions in the study, CU Boulder students had a similar reported commute time but traveled greater distances between locations throughout the day. A student might leave home to travel to the East Campus for work as a research assistant before heading to the central portion of campus for classes and studying at the library, and then end the day at practice for an athletic team. The geocoded data showed that while there were some outliers, student movements centered on the campus itself, suggesting that students' lives were primarily contained in the CU Boulder bubble (figure 4.1).

Choosing Where to Live

Student decisions about where to live were driven by many factors including cost, availability, environment, and convenience of location. The first-year students participating in the study indicated that they had little choice in their residence hall preference. Some chose to participate in a Residential Academic Program (RAP) that guaranteed them a room in a specific hall which often corresponded to their major or area of academic interest, such as engineering or global studies. Some students indicated they chose their current or former RAP based on the residence hall location, knowing it would be more convenient or offer additional amenities. The upperclassman research participants who discussed living on campus their first year often expressed frustration at the challenges of living in the residence halls. These frustrations included residing in a location far from classes, having little control in selecting roommates, and living in a disruptive environment.

Since a majority of CU Boulder students move to off-campus housing after their first year, this study shed light on how our students select off-campus housing. Rental costs were one major factor in this decision-making process, but students also considered the number of roommates, commuting options such as bike paths and public transportation, and proximity to campus, including the characteristics of the neighborhoods. For one student, living close to campus was of highest importance when selecting a living location, but she indicated that she worked longer hours so that she could afford to pay for the apartment. This student reported spending very little time socializing or participating in extracurricular activities, and a majority of her time was spent in class, studying, or working. For others, financially feasible housing close to campus meant living with upward of eight roommates where their personal space was not much bigger than a closet. These students prioritized proximity and cost effectiveness over a quiet or spacious home environment.

Several students noted selecting housing based on neighborhood for proximity not just to campus, but to where a majority of their classes are held.

For students in the College of Arts & Sciences, courses are primarily held on the western portion of campus compared to courses in engineering or business, which are situated on the eastern edge. As students progress in their college careers and are primarily enrolled in major courses, class locations are more likely to be situated in the areas of campus related to their college. This sentiment was echoed by numerous students, and many cited choosing to live on the side of campus based on where their disciplines were concentrated.

Others noted choosing locations farther away from campus for reasons related to cost and atmosphere. The neighborhood approximately three miles south of the campus is a mix of university students and community residents and tends to attract more graduate students. One student said that she chose that location because it was more affordable and provided a quieter environment desired by her and her roommates. For this student, these benefits far outweighed the challenges of this locale, which involved traveling farther to get to campus. Two transfer students lived in a town approximately fifteen miles away due to the significantly lower cost of living there. These financially independent, returning students noted that by residing outside of Boulder, they were able to moderate the number of hours worked and devote more time to their studies, despite longer commutes.

Commuting to and Around Campus

Where students chose to live impacted the time spent commuting and the transportation method used for getting to and around campus. Students who resided in centrally located residence halls or secured off-campus housing adjacent to the campus reported making more stops home during the day. These students would go between the campus for class and their residence halls or apartments for meals and studying before heading to work or other activities in the evening. Yet for some on-campus students, returning home was difficult due to their residence hall location. First-year student residence halls can be found interspersed with academic buildings in the center of the campus, sitting on the edge of the campus, and located in the resident academic village approximately a mile and a half from the center of the campus. As one student described it, "main campus is downtown and Kittredge is like the suburbs, and Will Vill is . . . the boondocks." For those students who reside in the "boondocks," there were fewer reported stops throughout the day, and upperclassman participants who had resided there in their first year mentioned that their commutes were less complicated now that they had moved off campus. One sophomore student noted about her off-campus apartment:

> I'm super centrally located, there's no reason for me not to get to class, my classes are basically closer living where I am now than living on campus, which is kind of funny.

We do not often think of on-campus students having a commute, but the ways that participants discussed their time, current or past, living in residence halls reinforced the complexity of navigating a large college campus.

Since a majority of participants reside in close proximity to the campus, driving was not a preferred commuting option, and commutes often involved multiple methods of transportation including bus, bicycle, and walking. Commutes were further complicated by other factors such as class schedule and other commitments including work, internships, or extracurricular activities. Limitations on parking meant that those students who did drive to campus must either purchase an expensive parking permit, pay an hourly rate at a meter that only allows for two to four hours of parking, or locate free city parking at a more distant location. One student who traveled from the more distant town attempted to purchase a parking permit only to find out that none were available. His solution was to park in a neighborhood adjacent to campus and then bike from there: "I just throw my bike in my truck and ride to campus, ride back [to my truck]." Others living in more distant neighborhoods mentioned that while they did not drive to campus, they sometimes relied on friends or roommates who do have a car and a parking permit.

Students also utilized local and regional buses to get to campus and around town. The Boulder area has a robust bus system, and students are provided with a free pass for the regional transit system. Additionally, the campus provides shuttles to the East Campus and Will Vill in order to assist students and researchers to travel to these outlying locations. While students mentioned using the campus shuttles, they noted that they only relied on these forms of transportation during inclement weather. One student residing outside of Boulder depended on the regional buses to get from home to campus and then to Denver. She noted that she kept her bike on campus because she was not guaranteed a spot on the bus to transport her bike, and she needed it to traverse the large campus when she only had ten minutes between classes. This student also indicated that she scheduled her classes to limit the number of days she came to campus. By restricting her classes to three days out of the week, she was able to limit her commuting to campus and better balance her time between work and school. Most students reported walking and biking as their main forms of transportation, since the town and campus are most friendly to these forms. However, many noted that using these forms of transportation had their own limitations, mostly in how long it took to get from one part of campus to another. Students echoed the sentiment that after their first few semesters on campus, they learned not to take classes back to back since the ten- or fifteen-minute breaks between classes did not allot enough time to travel between points.

While many students reported fairly short commutes by bus, bike, or walking from home to campus, a handful of students indicated that on days other than when the study was conducted, they may travel farther due to internship or work opportunities. One student whose academic day for the study looked like the typical CU Boulder bubble, indicated in the interview that on two other days of the week he drove twenty miles to the health sciences campus for an internship that lasted from 7:00 A.M. to 1:00 P.M. This student's internship days looked drastically different than his typical class days and were often more hectic, since he had to return to Boulder in time for an afternoon class and then immediately go to work off campus that evening. Other students noted that they pursued work and internship opportunities in Denver, approximately twenty miles away, because the opportunity was too good to pass up. But this meant longer, more complex commutes whether they drove to their destination or took public transportation.

How Commutes Impact Academic Work

Where students lived and with whom they lived had a strong impact on how and where they conducted their academic work. Only one participant indicated studying while commuting to campus on a regional bus, a 45-minute ride from a town fifteen miles away. This student often carried numerous bags for the day containing schoolwork materials and other personal items. She noted that she tried to prepare for the bus ride by downloading materials onto her laptop since there is no Wi-Fi, or she chose to focus on work that did not require a laptop such as language class homework. This student noted that while she preferred to use her commute time to complete academic work, it could be difficult due to insufficient space to carry out the tasks.

> I've had situations where I can't work on the thing I was going to work on because I need a book open and I need my laptop, multiple things, I have my lap and I have a backpack on my lap and I have my feet but I can't move them because I have my pannier . . . sometimes it's a little challenging.

While this student preferred to use her commute time for doing academic work and preparing for the day's classes, the heavily used commuter bus did not provide enough space to contain her personal belongings and still have enough room to bring out materials needed to study.

For the two students who lived in an even more distant town, the library served as one of their primary locations to conduct academic work both due to its location on campus and the services it provided. One noted that she acquired a locker in the library after she saw them in the corner of the first floor and inquired with the circulation desk about their availability. Campus affiliates can check out these lockers on a semester basis, which this commuter student mentioned as providing a space to store personal items and books, reducing the amount she carried with her on a daily basis. The location is convenient, since she uses that library location for her studying and the locker allowed her access to schoolbooks and materials without having to carry them around all day. The other student noted:

> I work from one to five [in the morning], so then from there I go to Norlin, the library here 'cause it's open twenty-four hours, which is pretty sweet and then I do some homework for two and a half, three hours or whichever time I have left before class.

For these students, the library provided services not otherwise found on campus. Other campus buildings do not open until later in the morning, and for off-campus students, the only other early-morning options are some dining halls or the recreation center, both of which cost additional fees to use. Because the library information commons was open twenty-four hours a day, this student with an alternative work schedule had a place to conduct academic work prior to his classes. This area also contains a microwave and other useful amenities for someone who often brings their own food to campus.

Whether the students who live in close proximity to campus return home throughout the day depended on a number of factors including home environment, number of roommates, and preferred study setting. Some students carried everything with them for the entire day, often leaving home by 9:00 A.M. and not returning until late in the evening. Sometimes this was due to extracurricular activities and employment, while other times it was due to not having a conducive study environment at home. These students noted that campus libraries served as frequently visited spaces between classes and other commitments. One student who regularly spent all day on campus in spite of living in close proximity exclaimed that:

> I was really excited when I learned you can check out textbooks at the library here, that was really awesome . . . that should be a thing for like every single class because boy does that make my life easier.

Not having to carry heavy textbooks or worry about forgetting the book needed at home saved this student physical and mental stress. Others noted that roommates and a lack of dedicated study space at home meant that they relied on the library for a space to conduct focused work. They usually sought out library study rooms or spaces designated as quiet zones, citing that the presence of others engaged in work encouraged them to complete their own work rather than socialize with friends.

Those who primarily studied at home shared two characteristics: a dedicated study space and fewer than two roommates. One student mentioned that her most productive place to study was at home since she had it set up with markers, highlighters, notebooks, and everything else she needed, including textbooks; she noted her frustration when she went to study elsewhere only to discover that a book or other course material she needed was left at home.

Three students indicated that their roommates shared their major and often had classes in common and could assist one another with their work. Being at home with food, having a study partner, and not worrying about leaving personal items unguarded were cited as strong reasons for studying at home.

For students who preferred to study later at night, the issue of parking could be problematic. Some student participants reported not wanting to walk long distances across campus and city neighborhoods at night, and the available parking was expensive and inconvenient, causing them to locate alternatives for their main study locations. One student noted that rather than going to the library, she would study in a common room located in an academic building at the edge of campus. This area had free parking after 7:00 P.M. and was located adjacent to the building. Students who lived in residence halls in the "boondocks" felt it was easier to study in their academic village rather than traverse the campus.

BARRIERS AND FRUSTRATIONS THAT STUDENTS ENCOUNTER

Our study of the daily lives of our students provided us with a better under-standing of how to approach removing these barriers and frustrations we were already aware of. Students discussed spending time between classes try-ing to study, usually in the library, but it was often difficult to locate a place that suited their needs. The students wanted space to spread out since they were often using books, notebooks, and a computer to complete their aca-demic work. Additionally, these students often desired quiet spaces to engage in focused academic work and expressed frustration at not locating a space in an area that was quiet, or because other students would be making noise in what were perceived to be quiet areas. Our participants all seemed to have study locations they used repeatedly, primarily in the main library, that they had found when they first used the library, and they were unaware of other study spaces in the large, maze-like building.

Access to electrical outlets was key for the students since they often charged multiple devices: all of our library locations suffer from lack of elec-trical outlets. Students noted that it was frustrating to locate a prime study space only to discover they did not have access to an electrical outlet or they had left their charger at home. Some participants noted that they relied on library computers since theirs might be old and inefficient or they were too heavy to carry around all day. The library has reduced the number of available computer terminals over the past few years, and students noticed that there were fewer stations and longer waits.

INTERVENTIONS AND INITIATIVES

We used information gleaned from the study to bolster existing services, make adjustments to learning spaces, and lay the foundation for new initiatives. Through these students' lives we were able to see the complexity of the day-to-day student experience and how commuting to and around campus was an important factor.

This study highlighted that students were unaware of many library resources and services regardless of the time they spent conducting academic work in the library. Many library users would benefit from long-standing services like course reserves. Since this term does not resonate with students, we are examining how to market reserves in a more approachable way. We are working with our communications team to devise a strategy to highlight this service, and to partner with instructors to stress the importance of making course materials available through reserves. We are also discussing open resources as an alternative. This study highlights how materials on course reserves assist students in completing their academic work for a variety of reasons, including reducing financial costs or making materials available without their having to remember each text or being limited in the amount they carry with them.

Additionally, one library location checks out cell phone and laptop chargers for limited use, usually set for two hours. Study participants who were heavy library users noted the frustration of limited access to electrical outlets and of leaving chargers at home, yet none were aware that the library provided chargers and power strips for checkout. However, this service is not available at other library locations across campus, and we are exploring how to expand the checkout of commonly used chargers.

The University Libraries are currently examining ways to expand the availability of lockers. Even without any advertising about their location, availability, or purpose, the lockers are full each semester, and at times have a waiting list. Further investigation found that there are scant opportunities on campus for students to lock up their belongings. No other buildings on campus provide access to lockers without a fee or membership in a specific college or department. The libraries are investigating possible locations and alternative reservation procedures for additional lockers. Options include making some lockers available for daily use only, placing some in the learning commons portion of the main library which has 24-hour access, and expanding the service to branch locations.

Information gathered from the research participants combined with other user assessments has driven furniture purchase decisions and space enhancements. To solve the problem of insufficient seating across all libraries, there has been a recent effort to adjust underutilized spaces and consider how other spaces in the libraries might be reimagined to provide additional learning environments for users. For example, the learning commons area was able to purchase new furniture that included tables with integrated power outlets. The original layout for the learning commons was to have flexible seating in order to encourage collaborative learning, and over time, we determined that students were looking for more individual work spaces even in an area that has a louder noise level. By reimagining the space, we have been able to increase seating capacity, retain some of the flexible seating features, and add in furniture that meets the needs of how our users work. While lounge seating was included as part of the original design, we paired them with large tables to provide needed work space.

Since this study was conducted, the libraries have undertaken an initiative to craft signage to indicate quiet and group work spaces across all locations. Library spaces have been zoned based on feedback from students and library staff familiar with the areas. The zones are still in a testing phase, so they can be adjusted as we observe student use and can make improvements to the signage. As these zones are finalized, we are working to craft maps of each library location, indicating different zones available so that users can locate spaces conducive to the work they need to engage in. While creating the zones in the Norlin Library, there was debate surrounding how much of the spaces needed to be zoned for collaborative work. Using information gleaned from this study, reinforced with observation of user behavior, provided the argument to zone more spaces for quiet individualized work.

CONCLUSIONS AND NEXT STEPS

For students who conducted their academic work in alternate locations other than home or the library, it was illuminating to learn about these preferred study spaces. While some of these preferences were driven by noise level or crowding, other factors pushed students to use alternate spaces. For those who cited parking or walking across campus later in the day as barriers to using the library, we can assess how the library might fit into the identified alternate spaces. We cannot solve the campus parking issue, but we can think of the other spaces available to students for their academic work and think of how we might highlight library resources and services in those spaces. For example, the resident academic village recently opened a new dining hall that incorporates student support services such as health care and tutoring. The library could partner with these existing student support efforts to promote library resources and services and test initiatives such as peer-to-peer reference support. Since the residence halls in this area are comprised of mainly first-year students, this could be an opportunity to connect with students and emphasize the value of the library as more than just a physical location on the other side of campus.

This study has also left us asking new questions about our students. Future plans include examining the commutes of the 4,000 undergraduate students living outside of Boulder in order to gain an understanding of the decisions and challenges of residing outside of the bubble. This study demonstrated that on-campus students can face more complicated commutes than those off campus. In what ways can the library play a role in supporting student academic work when physical locations are not in close proximity to the residence hall? We are exploring increased offerings aimed at first-year students in order to promote library spaces and services and better understand the needs of incoming students. As the campus grows to other locations such as the CU South expansion, we will need to address the question of how the library fits into these spaces. Some CU Boulder librarians are partnering with our transfer student office, and study results are informing their initiatives and research questions. Even more so, the results from this study remind us that student lives are complex and that they are often negotiating multiple identities in their time as students, regardless of whether or not their commutes take them beyond the campus bubble.

REFERENCES

Asher, Andrew, Juliann Couture, Jean Amaral, Maura Smale, Sarah Lowe, Donna Lanclos, Mariana Regalado, and Barbara Fister. 2017. "A Day in the Life: Practical Strategies for Understanding Student Space-Use Practices." In *Proceedings of the 2016 Library Assessment Conference: Building Effective, Sustainable, Practical Assessment, October 31–November 2, 2016, Arlington, VA,* edited by Sue Baughman, Steve Hiller, Katie Monroe, and Angela Pappalardo, 428–38. Washington, DC: Association of Research Libraries. http://libraryassessment .org/archive/conference-proceedings-2016.shtml.

Brown-Sica, Margaret S. 2012. "Library Spaces for Urban, Diverse Commuter Students: A Participatory Action Research Project." *College & Research Libraries* 73 (3): 217–31. doi:10.5860/crl-221.

Delcore, Henry D., James Mullooly, and Michael Scroggins. 2009. *The Library Study at Fresno State.* Fresno, CA: Institute of Public Anthropology, California State University. www.fresnostate.edu/socialsciences/anthropology/documents/ipa/ TheLibraryStudy(DelcoreMulloolyScroggins).pdf.

Duke, Lynda M., and Andrew D. Asher, eds. 2012. *College Libraries and Student Culture: What We Now Know.* Chicago: American Library Association.

Foster, Nancy Fried, and Susan L. Gibbons, eds. 2007. *Studying Students: The Undergraduate Research Project at the University of Rochester.* Chicago: Association of College & Research Libraries.

Huron Education. 2015. "CU Boulder Space Utilization and Optimization Final Report." University of Colorado Boulder Capital Asset Management. www .colorado.edu/capital-asset-management/sites/default/files/attached-files/cu_ boulder_space_utilization_and_optimization_final_report_august_2015.pdf.

Regalado, Mariana, and Maura A. Smale. 2015. "'I Am More Productive in the Library Because It's Quiet': Commuter Students in the College Library." *College & Research Libraries* 76 (7): 899–913. doi:10.5860/cr1.76.7.899.

University of Colorado Boulder. 2017a. "Common Data Set 2016–17." www.colorado .edu/oda/sites/default/files/attached-files/cds_2016–2017_temp.pdf.

———. 2017b. "Estimates of Where CU Boulder Students Live." https://public .tableau.com/profile/university.of.colorado.boulder.ir#!/vizhome/students_live/ ByZipCode.

U.S. Department of Housing and Urban Development. 2017. "Comprehensive Housing Market Analysis: Boulder, Colorado." https://www.huduser.gov/portal/ publications/pdf/BoulderCO-comp-17.pdf.

JEAN AMARAL,
MARIANA REGALADO, and
MAURA A. SMALE

5
A Decade of Research at Urban Commuter Colleges

At the City University of New York (CUNY), the largest public urban university system in the United States, almost all students are commuters: 93 percent commute by subway, bus, train, walking, bike, and ferry, in order of prevalence, while only 7 percent commute by car (CUNY OIRA 2017). Commuting is a defining characteristic for much of the CUNY community, and is integral to understanding the lived experience of CUNY students. To better serve our students, we need to understand how commuting impacts their college experience and day-to-day lives. What library tools help them do their research from off campus? Where do they find the time and space to do their schoolwork? If they are not using our libraries, where are they doing their academic work? In what ways can the library better serve our students?

Since 2009 we have been engaged in qualitative studies at seven CUNY campuses to explore how, where, when, and with what tools our undergraduates do their academic work. We have learned about how students move through their days in New York City as scholars, workers, caregivers, and community members. Students have shared with us their strategies for writing papers during long commutes, finding a quiet spot in the library or on campus to study, supplementing college library resources with those of their local public libraries, and using their smartphones for research at all hours of the day and night. Our long-term perspective has enabled us to consider change over time, and has revealed unexpected similarities in the student experiences across both community and baccalaureate colleges in our university system. Our research into the lived experience of CUNY students has also profoundly impacted us as practitioners and informs the totality of our work at our libraries, from space allocation and renovation plans to implementing new technology initiatives to information literacy, instruction, and beyond.

INSTITUTIONAL CONTEXT
The City University of New York

Serving almost 275,000 students at 24 undergraduate and graduate schools across New York City, CUNY's mission is to provide equal access to education for traditionally underserved populations whose remarkable diversity is apparent in student demographics. In 2016, among undergraduates across the university, 42 percent came from families with an annual household income of less than $20,000 and 71 percent came from families with income under $40,000, while 45 percent were first-generation college students. CUNY is a majority minority institution: the system-wide self-reported ethnicity of undergraduates in 2016 was 31 percent Hispanic, 26 percent black, 22 percent white, and 20 percent Asian/Pacific Islander (CUNY OIRA 2017).

The CUNY system is large and complex. While a central university administration does provide some services and resources and set some policy for the entire system, each CUNY campus has its own administration, faculty, and physical plant, as well as its own unique campus culture. Some CUNY colleges draw students primarily from the surrounding geographical area, while others attract students from across the city. The undergraduate institutions at CUNY include nine senior colleges that grant baccalaureate degrees, seven community colleges that grant associate degrees, and four comprehensive colleges that grant both associate and baccalaureate degrees. Many of the senior and comprehensive colleges also offer master's programs. While several of the senior colleges do have a residence hall, each dorm houses less than 5 percent of students at that campus.

Our research has encompassed seven CUNY campuses, including three senior colleges: Brooklyn College (BC), the City College of New York (CCNY), and Hunter College (HC); three community colleges: Bronx Community College (BCC), Borough of Manhattan Community College (BMCC), and Queensborough Community College (QCC); and one comprehensive college: New York City College of Technology (City Tech or CT) (table 5.1). These include the colleges where we work as well as colleges that we selected because they represent a broad cross-section of community and senior colleges at CUNY. There is also a variety of campus layouts across CUNY campuses; some have a traditional quadrangle layout around outdoor spaces for student use, while

TABLE 5.1

Undergraduate enrollment and college attributes at CUNY college research sites, Fall 2016 (CUNY OIRA 2017)

SCHOOL	DEGREE/TYPE	UNDERGRADUATE ENROLLMENT	CAMPUS TYPE	LIBRARY FT²
BC	senior college	~13,500	traditional	197,000
BCC	community college	~10,000	traditional	57,084
BMCC	community college	~25,500	vertical	52,000
CCNY	senior college	~12,600	traditional	175,000
CT	comprehensive college	~16,000	vertical	40,000
HC	senior college	~15,600	vertical	160,000
QCC	community college	~13,500	traditional	38,214

others have a more urban feel and are primarily vertical, consisting of high-rise buildings with little outdoor space. Students at the community colleges represent a wide range, from those just out of high school enrolled in a liberal arts degree program, to those focused on certification for entry into professional careers, to returning students gathering credits needed for entry into baccalaureate or graduate programs. At the CUNY senior colleges as much as 75 percent of the undergraduate student body is made up of students who have transferred in, primarily from CUNY community colleges (Wrigley 2010, 2).

RESEARCH STUDIES AND METHODS

The three authors of this chapter are all faculty librarians at CUNY, and as tenure line faculty we engage in scholarly research and publishing. Our research questions have developed out of our experiences as practicing librarians and are informed by our training, reviews of the literature, and interactions with other researcher-practitioners, rather than via institutional mandate to investigate particular issues or concerns in our libraries. While we have selected these research projects based on our own interests and experience, we are eager to use the results in our libraries.

CUNY students have been the main focus of our studies, rather than the library. Our research has sought to uncover how our students constitute their academic lives given that they spend substantial amounts of time away from campus and are typically negotiating myriad life roles. We have developed a deeper understanding of our students and their experiences, and our long-term perspective enables us to see how changes in our libraries, technology, the colleges, and higher education have impacted the student experience.

To reach students from across our campuses in our research projects, especially students who might not be library users, we have relied on convenience samples, recruiting via flyers hung around campus, with most displayed outside of the library. Our research with CUNY students encompasses a range of distinct research questions we have asked students.[1] Across the different studies, questions, and methods, our overarching, guiding inquiry has been: how, when, where, and with what tools do our undergraduates do their academic work? In particular, we have been very interested as to how the library fits in for students—or not. To explore the student experience, we have employed a variety of open-ended prompts to elicit detailed responses from students and faculty. All of the studies we describe were approved by the CUNY Institutional Review Board.

Undergraduate Scholarly Habits Study

Inspired by the library study at Rochester (Foster and Gibbons 2007) and using similar ethnographic techniques, Smale and Regalado began a pilot study at City Tech and Brooklyn College in 2009/10 which they expanded in 2010/11 to four additional campuses—BMCC, Bronx CC, City College, and Hunter College. Our research questions were: How do students study, research, and complete their assignments? Where and how do students do their coursework in the context of their days? In two of our interview methods, we asked students to think about their experiences before we interviewed them by having them map their days on campus or photograph items related to schoolwork, and bring these artifacts to the interview for discussion. We also asked students about how they completed a research project from start to finish using retrospective research process interviews, and to draw or sketch the process while they spoke. These photographs and hand drawings by students enrich our data because they visually demonstrate the varying importance of activities, friends, objects, means, and the general environment. To provide context for the student experience, we interviewed faculty at these campuses about their expectations for student work on research assignments. These interviews yielded rich data about the gratifications and frustrations students encountered and gave us new insights into the student experience, including a heightened appreciation of the central place of technology.

Information Needs and Information-Seeking

After learning about the Ethnographic Research in Illinois Academic Libraries (ERIAL) Project (Duke and Asher 2012), Amaral began a study in 2013 at QCC focused on two research questions: What information needs do community college students and faculty have? How do students and faculty seek information in relation to those needs? Three methods were used for gathering data: questionnaires, seven-day information diaries, and two sets of interviews: one with students who completed information diaries, and the second with students demonstrating their personal learning technology environments, including resources they used in their learning. While most of the students in this study viewed the library favorably, many did not use its services. The role the library played in their information-seeking was often minimal, especially after the students completed English Composition and Introduction to Speech, the two courses that most frequently took advantage of library instruction. The results also highlighted that much of the information these community college students needed to be successful in their academic and professional lives was generally not found through library resources.

The Future Library

After taking a position at BMCC, Amaral began a research project in 2015/16 addressing the conclusion from her prior information needs and information seeking study that the community college library is often peripheral to students. The research questions for this study were: In 2030, what resources and services would an urban community college library provide that would ensure it is filling an essential role for students, faculty, and the institution? What steps would need to be taken between the present and 2030 to achieve this vision of the library? Data was gathered from focus groups with administrators, staff, librarians, faculty, and most importantly, students; there were five student focus groups with twenty-four total participants. Student responses focused on technology, space, and the library as connector. They also implicitly identified a need to shift to a student-centered library, similar to the shift in classrooms to student-centered learning. Participants across all focus groups frequently mentioned that the library should be an inviting community center, bringing together students, faculty, staff, and the local community. Additionally, there was a desire for the future library to move from a transactional space and services to an experiential space and relational services.

Student Technology Use

To refresh our data on student use of technology for their schoolwork, and to draw on our combined prior qualitative research, we three collaborated on a research project at BMCC, Brooklyn College, and City Tech in 2015/16. Research questions included: What technologies are students using for coursework in and out of class, as well as on and off campus? How are they using the technologies? What barriers and affordances do students encounter in their technology use? We conducted expeditious in-person interviews, tabling at a busy area on all three campuses, as well as sending a questionnaire about technology use to students in hybrid and online classes in Fall 2015. In Spring 2016 we sent a similar questionnaire to faculty teaching hybrid and online classes about their own experiences using technology in these courses.

A Day in the Life

In 2015 we three also joined colleagues at five other colleges and universities from across the country for a collaborative, multi-site mapping project titled "A Day in the Life" and intended to gather holistic information about the complexity of students' life contexts and better understand how to develop university programs, services, and resources that effectively address students' needs (Asher et al. 2017). Students from BMCC, Brooklyn College, and City Tech participated in this research along with students from a wide cross-section of institutions: urban and suburban, commuter and residential, and community colleges through research universities. Our aim was to construct detailed maps of students' days, including locations and activities. Student participants were sent a three-question survey—Where are you? What are you doing? How do you feel?—via text message at fixed times over the course of a single day. A map of each student's day was generated from the responses, which were discussed with students during follow-up interviews. This research updated our understanding of how CUNY students spend their days. We have noted a number of changes in how students use our facilities and get their work done, and in particular we heard about greater use of mobile technology on the commute for their academic work than we did in 2009/11.

Student Reading Practices

Most recently, in 2017 Smale began a new round of open-ended interviews with students at BMCC, Brooklyn College, and City Tech about their academic reading habits. The research questions for this study were: How do students get access to their course readings? How do students accomplish and prioritize doing the reading both within the context of their total course load and within the full landscape of their busy schedules? The semi-structured interviews explored student attitudes and practices with regard to their course readings. These interviews have produced much insight into how students acquire and access their course readings, including their consideration of the cost of course materials. They have also shed light on factors students consider when balancing time spent on course reading with their other academic and nonacademic commitments.

Data Analysis

Our studies have used a range of qualitative research methods, and the data we have gathered includes audio, images (photos and drawings), and text. With the exception of the brief technology interviews in which we tabled at a busy area on campus, all individual and focus group interviews were recorded using a digital voice recorder, and the audio files were transcribed to text. We have used two qualitative software platforms—ATLAS.ti and Dedoose—to code the transcribed interview data and facilitate the analysis of relevant themes from the data. We have benefited from research leave provided to faculty by our university as well as a number of small grants that enabled us to offer incentives for student participants and hire research assistants to assist with the transcription.[2]

RESULTS AND FINDINGS

Between our various studies, we have met in person with over 340 CUNY students from whom we collected hundreds of hours of transcribed interviews and dozens of drawings and photographs; received questionnaire responses from over 2,300 students; and plotted out many miles of movement through their days. We have learned much about their experiences, knowledge that has astonished and delighted us as well as occasionally caused us concern or frustration on their behalf. The students we interviewed also often expressed surprise, pleasure, and even remorse at their own habits or constraints. We found that the more depth required by the interview method, the more likely students were to express appreciation for the opportunity to reflect on and consider their own practices.

Despite the differences between the seven colleges in our study noted above, we have been intrigued to find that the students we met across CUNY described remarkably similar experiences in their home, academic, and work environments. Their common challenges encompassed navigating their commutes, negotiating shared spaces at home and on campus, managing their access to technology, and grappling with technology inadequacies and failures. Indeed, we found that many differences were more dependent on the quality and quantity of campus facilities and resources than on whether students attended a community college or a senior college. Students showed us they were eager to learn and do well, despite the many obstacles they encountered as commuter students with multiple life roles. Across our various interview types and questions, we have identified two themes that are most useful for us as practicing academic librarians at commuter institutions: students' information needs and the importance of time.

Student Academic Practices

As librarians, we are naturally very interested in student information needs and information-seeking experiences, and how these are impacted by students' multiple life roles, by their access to spaces on campus and at home, and by their commuter status. In particular we found that student experiences clustered around structure, feedback and support, the place of libraries, and the impact of technology and time on information-seeking.

While our student participants recognized the importance of structure in organizing their academic work, they were also resistant to it. Students told us how little they liked it when their instructors provided (or imposed) scaffolding, deadlines, or library instruction sessions, yet they also acknowledged the benefits of these and other structures as helpful in guiding them toward successful assignment completion. In particular, students framed structure as a tool to fight procrastination, while referencing their multiple roles as students, employees, caregivers, and more, with their concomitant time constraints. As one City Tech student noted appreciatively about the scaffolding of the final project for his English composition course, "You couldn't procrastinate on it."

The most successful students told us that they actively sought feedback and support, not only from faculty, but also from tutors, peers, friends, and family members. Students also noted a lack of feedback from some faculty, while other students were able to take advantage of office hours to receive feedback and ask questions. Many students did not seek feedback, as faculty lamented, often citing reluctance to bother their instructor, a past experience when an instructor was dismissive, or office hours that conflicted with other important commitments. Tutoring centers were another source for feedback on assignments and even on take-home exams, as well as for help with the course material and concepts. Classmates and friends emerged as an important source of feedback and support, with students texting and e-mailing questions to each other as well as meeting face-to-face, as one QCC student related: "I e-mail my friends and say I'm having a problem with this or I'm not sure how to do that." Classmates might provide feedback in class, as well as outside of it, with students forming study groups. Students also mentioned family members who provided feedback and assistance—both parents and siblings.

Student information-seeking practices were of particular interest to us, especially library use. In fact, few students told us that their information needs were successfully met by the library. Lack of awareness of library resources was a major barrier, as were access issues and the complexity of most library tools, including difficulty logging in or deciphering database results. Some students found public libraries to be friendlier and more helpful; many had used their neighborhood public libraries often while in high school. One of the greatest course information needs met by the college library was for the textbook, since all of the campuses had at least some textbooks on reserve. However, students had to find the time to use library reserves, which was often challenging given their complicated schedules. Some students told us they found that digital versions of, or alternatives to, their textbooks saved them both time and money.

Many students reported that they were more successful on the Web than in the library for their academic information needs, including faculty recommendations to supplement course materials and explain difficult concepts or summarize required readings. Students mentioned coding and language websites, videos, and other online tutorials, with some searching for duplicative information to verify the first source they found. Students' experiences using the Web for nonacademic information needs informed their ideas about research and reflected needs that may have directly impacted their ability to be successful in their courses. These needs ranged from entertainment to food and housing insecurity to family mental illness, among others. Given that many of their information needs were not served by the library, it is understandable that students defaulted to web searching for both academic and nonacademic needs.

In addition to prior comfort and habit with the Web, students' information-seeking practices were driven by technology. When we first interviewed students in 2009, few had smartphones; many cobbled together a combination of feature phones and iPod touches or smartphones without a data plan for Wi-Fi access on the go. By 2015 when we asked students about their college-related technology experiences, every student respondent had a mobile phone, and most had smartphones that some used a great deal for schoolwork. Combined with increased access to Wi-Fi, including throughout most subway stations in New York City, students took advantage of smartphones (and tablets) to do their coursework anytime and anywhere. While the most common activity was reading, students also researched and wrote papers on mobile devices or used their smartphones in class for quick lookups. A number of students described using their phones to do research for papers while in bed. Along with the affordances technology provided, there were also drawbacks to technology use for students. Students talked about the learning management system and other applications not working well on mobile devices, as well as weak and spotty Wi-Fi on campuses, among other issues. Faculty also noted that students' use of mobile technology may be less than ideal for learning and successfully completing academic assignments, yet mobile is only likely to become more important over time.

Time as a Facilitator and Constraint for Students

The theme of time ran as an undercurrent through all CUNY student experiences. Given their many life roles, the students we met were practiced multitaskers who were adept at making the most of time in their busy schedules to do their academic work. As a BMCC student noted: "Even when I'm taking lunch or breakfast, I'm usually reading." At the same time, students experienced factors beyond their control that constrained their time and could interfere with their ability to complete their academic work.

The commute was a prominent feature of students' experiences with time management. The average commute for CUNY students is 45 to 60 minutes each way, typically via New York City's subways and buses (CUNY OIRA 2012). Robust public transportation enabled many CUNY students to optimize their time on the commute, and most students did at least some of their academic work while traveling. While a common academic activity on the commute was reading—both on paper and mobile devices—students also told us they used their mobile devices for research using Internet or library resources, e-mailing instructors, and writing papers and assignments. Using the commute time efficiently was important to many students, including one from City Tech who noted:

> First time in college, I didn't realize how difficult it would be for a college student to study, so, like, I figured instead of listening to music and having my headphones plugged in, I'd rather study on the subway. I noticed how my grades improved since I've been doing that.

Students found that multitasking on the commute could be challenging. Subways and buses are heavily used in New York City and can be very crowded, especially during rush hour; many students told us that they were unable to do their coursework on a subway or bus if they did not have a seat and the personal space that a seat affords. Notably, some students invested time to prepare for the commute by scanning or downloading and then uploading course readings in advance so that these materials could be read without Internet access. Wi-Fi coverage in the subway system is not yet complete, especially in tunnels between stations. On buses and above-ground subway lines, students can use a data plan to access the Internet on their smartphones, though this may carry an additional cost that students may find untenable.

CUNY students employed a variety of strategies to optimize the spaces they were in during the time they had available. Most students preferred to do their coursework in their campus library, citing it as a quiet, distraction-free place for their work. Students also used library resources like reserve textbooks and computers, as well as study space. Many students especially appreciated carrel desks for the privacy they afford, privacy that could be a struggle to achieve at home, where they often lived with several other people. Alternatively, some students appreciated the support of family members when they did their academic work at home, and preferred to study there. Others were able to use some time and space at their workplaces in order to do schoolwork, or they used the public library for research and studying.

Despite the variety of locations available to students to do their studying and assignments, many struggled to find an appropriate place during the time available to them. An hours-long break between classes to read and do home-work might be thwarted if their campus library was too crowded or noisy for them to concentrate. Other delays they encountered at the library included limited two-hour loans for reserve books and long lines at photocopiers or scanners. Our libraries at CUNY are not typically open after 11:00 P.M. (nor are public libraries), and work and family commitments meant that some students were doing their academic work when the libraries were already closed for the day. Yet some students found the campus and library to be so advantageous for their schoolwork that they would commute to campus even on days when they did not have classes, just so they could study in the college library. While we have been glad to learn of their appreciation of the library, commuting into campus on a day without courses or other commitments is an investment of time that was not possible for all students.

Students tended to characterize their experiences with technology along a continuum of time. At one end were those technologies that allowed students to save time. These included activities such as using mobile devices to engage with schoolwork on the commute, doing research on their phone when siblings were using the family computer, or accessing a computer on campus between classes. Students very much appreciated how technology allowed them to quickly check due dates or get reminders for approaching deadlines.

At the other end of the intersection of time and technology were experiences that caused students to lose or waste time. Some of these were readily acknowledged by students to be their own challenges, such as wasting time on social media, or forgetting to bring the charger for their laptop to campus. However, much of the time-wasting that students reported was characterized by them as technology failures outside of their control. Campus Wi-Fi could be so slow as to be unusable, or one or another university enterprise system was down, in particular the learning management system. Students reported frustrations with lines to print out an assignment or paper that they wrote on the commute, or to print online reading that they needed to be able to access offline. Understandably, students expressed frustration when the technologies they had hoped would enable their academic work at the times that were best for them instead wasted their time and added to their workload. We also heard from many students of their reluctance to ask for help to make the most of their time; most notably, students expressed widespread discomfort in requesting that computer lab managers or librarians moderate the noise levels and behavior of other students.

IMPACTS AND OUTCOMES

At CUNY being a commuter is a defining characteristic of the student experience. The college campus is only one place in, and their academic roles are only one aspect of, CUNY students' broader lives. From the beginning of our studies we have been interested to hear from our students about their campus and student experiences in order to better understand the role of the library and to help us consider how the library can better support them in their information-seeking and other academic needs. Our research has informed a number of changes—both specific and general—in space, services, and instruction at our libraries, as well as a change in our mindset as practicing academic librarians.

Our understanding of students' space needs on campus and how students use our library spaces has informed decisions about how we chose to change (or maintain) various spaces in our libraries. Perhaps most notable is our strong commitment to preserve—and, if at all possible, increase—quiet study spaces. Students have expressed much appreciation for the privacy of carrel desks, and we have successfully used this knowledge to resist the occasional efforts to remove this style of desk, which is sometimes viewed as outdated by stakeholders outside the library. Furthermore, hearing a wish from students for different kinds of spaces, quiet and for conversation, as well as learning that many students do not ask for help from librarians in controlling the use of space, has informed our decisions about adding and improving signage at all three libraries.

We have also learned much from our student interviews and questionnaires that has influenced our decisions about services in the library. Finding and using working printers on campus during the time students had available was a critical need highlighted throughout our studies. At Brooklyn College, student descriptions of frustrations encountered when printing out assignments before class galvanized our decisions to add dedicated print stations on the first floor of the library. While at certain peak times there are still lines to print, overall the quick print stations have been a success. At City Tech—where the library is more space-constrained than Brooklyn College—the decision was made to bring in a new system to offer wireless printing so that students can print from their own devices as well as library computers. Both BMCC and City Tech libraries now offer tablet computer loans for students; BMCC and Brooklyn College libraries also loan laptops, which City Tech's library plans to add in the near future. A clear student need for scanning capability to support studying on the commute encouraged a push for adding multiple free scanners at the Brooklyn College and BMCC libraries.

Our research with CUNY students has enabled insight into their experiences as whole people, not just as students, and we have also added services in our libraries tailored to the whole person. At Brooklyn College a Learning Center tutor now has office hours in the library, stationed by the reference desk in a small computer classroom. Knowledge of how disconnected students sometimes feel from the various services on campus ensured quick approval and strong support for the program, which has been very successful. In an effort to serve student needs beyond studying, relaxation stations, which include games and adult coloring among other activities, and music events were added at BMCC during midterms and finals, and students have responded positively. In informal feedback for the music events, 98 percent of respondents wanted more of them, often appreciating the stress relief they provided, as this student expressed: "The music was very soothing when I was under pressure, Thank you. It was wonderful, bravo!!" Other students suggested additional activities, including "how-to events based on crafts, like DIY (do-it-yourself) products, more music, and anything that is fun would be cool." Students appreciated the opportunities provided to take breaks, de-stress, and recharge for studying.

Inspired by how well students responded to the self-reflection inherent in the research process interviews, at Brooklyn College we have introduced a "draw your research steps" exercise in some instruction contexts for enhanced student reflection and learning (Georgas, Regalado, and Burgess 2017). Acknowledging widespread student experiences using Google and Wikipedia as starting points for research has led all three of us to place a greater emphasis on what students already know about research in our instruction sessions. BMCC librarians are also developing "Research for Life" workshops in collaboration with student success programs, such as Accelerated Study in Associate Programs (ASAP) and the BMCC Learning Academy, to address both academic and nonacademic information needs. At City Tech we have been able to use what we learned about students' busy schedules and use of technology for their academic work to make the case to add funding for 24/7 chat reference service to our library budget, which has helped us to better meet students' reference and instruction needs.

In addition to changes to library resources and services, we have found that we, ourselves, have been changed as a result of our near-decade of listening to students talk about their experiences. Unless we are teaching a semester-long course, the nature of our work as librarians is that we are most likely to meet students briefly, if sometimes intensively, to focus on their immediate research needs. We do not usually have the opportunity for sustained, regular contact with students, or the chance to get to know them very well. Our qualitative, ethnographically informed research methods and questions have given us insights into the broader student experience, and have helped us get to know CUNY students in a way that otherwise would not have been possible. We are grateful for every minute of our research because we loved meeting students and hearing their stories about their successes and challenges, information that has informed decision-making in our jobs and our libraries more broadly.

Since undertaking this research with CUNY students, we are more attuned to careful observation and listening as we see and interact with students studying in our libraries, using library services and resources, and attending library instruction sessions and workshops. In turn, our observations have guided new research questions and studies: our recent questionnaires about student technology use were inspired by our interactions with students doing the work for online courses in our library computer labs, as opposed to off campus, as is often assumed for students enrolled in these classes. Our research has also opened a conversation about the role and value of qualitative data in institutional planning in our libraries and on our campuses. We have had opportunities to connect with stakeholders across the university via the presentation and publication of our research, including college faculty and administrators, IT administrators, library faculty, campus centers for teaching and learning, and others interested in the CUNY student experience. We continue to advocate for improvements; our research has provided evidence that changes are needed, and can serve as a compelling accompaniment to the quantitative data we collect in our libraries and on campus.

Ultimately our research with students and faculty is greater than the sum of its parts. It has brought both intangible benefits and at the same time has transformed us and our experience as academic librarians. We have gained a new openness to hearing what students are saying about library services and beyond, to truly listening and understanding how decisions we make in the library or at the college directly impact them. Fundamental to this has been a shift in how we perceive our CUNY students. Rather than seeing them as only students, our research has helped us more fully embrace the reality that being students is only one part of their experience, only one of their multiple life-roles. Students and their academic success have always been our foundational mission; now we more clearly see students as partners, not only in their own successes, but also in ours.

REFERENCES

Asher, Andrew, Juliann Couture, Jean Amaral, Maura Smale, Sarah Lowe, Donna Lanclos, Mariana Regalado, and Barbara Fister. 2017. "A Day in the Life: Practical Strategies for Understanding Student Space-Use Practices." In *Proceedings of the 2016 Library Assessment Conference: Building Effective, Sustainable, Practical Assessment, October 31–November 2, 2016, Arlington, VA,* edited by Sue Baughman, Steve Hiller, Katie Monroe, and Angela Pappalardo, 428–38. Washington, DC: Association of Research Libraries. http://libraryassessment .org/archive/conference-proceedings-2016.shtml.

CUNY OIRA. 2012. "2012 Student Experience Survey." https://public.tableau.com/ views/2016StudentExperienceSurvey.

———. 2017. "2016 Student Experience Survey." Tableau Software. https://public .tableau .com/views/2016StudentExperienceSurvey/MainMenu?%3Aembed =y&%3AshowVizHome=no&%3Adisplay_count=y&%3Adisplay_static_image= y&%3AbootstrapWhenNotified=true.

Duke, Lynda M., and Andrew D Asher, eds. 2012. *College Libraries and Student Culture: What We Now Know.* Chicago: American Library Association.

Foster, Nancy F., and Susan Gibbons, ed. 2007. *Studying Students: The Undergraduate Research Project at the University of Rochester.* Chicago: Association of College & Research Libraries.

Georgas, Helen, Mariana Regalado, and Matthew Burgess. 2017. "Choose Your Own Adventure: The Hero's Journey and the Research Process." In *ACRL 2017 Conference Proceedings: At the Helm: Leading Transformation, March 22–25, Baltimore, Maryland,* edited by Dawn M. Mueller, 120–32. Chicago: Association of Research Libraries. www.ala.org/acrl/conferences/acrl2017/papers.

Wrigley, Julia. 2010. "Improving Student Transfer at CUNY." City University of New York. http://www2.cuny.edu/wp-content/uploads/sites/4/page-assets/about/administration/offices/undergraduate-studies/pathways/about/policies/policy-archive/Pathways_TransferReport.pdf.

NOTES

1. Our full research protocols for each of the methods described below are available on our project website (https://ushep.commons.gc.cuny.edu/project-design/) and at http://academicworks.cuny.edu/bm_pubs/64/, http://academicworks.cuny.edu/bm_pubs/66/, http://academicworks.cuny.edu/bm_pubs/68/, http://academicworks.cuny.edu/bm_pubs/70/, and http://academicworks.cuny.edu/bm_pubs/71/.

2. The Professional Staff Congress-City University of New York (PSC-CUNY) Research Award Program established by our labor union and university offers CUNY faculty the opportunity to apply for modest grants in support of research.

BRIAN GREENE and
ELIZABETH HORAN

6

"I Study in My Car"

Exploring the Study Habits of California
Community College Commuter Students

Essentially all of California's community college students are commuter students. Just eleven of the system's 114 institutions have small residence halls, and therefore nearly all of the system's two million students commute to class. Yet "commuter student" is not a label commonly associated with the students at our colleges, perhaps because it applies to everyone and thus is not especially descriptive. Even students do not identify themselves as "commuters," yet it is a label that fits (Badger 2014). Thinking about our students as commuter students might be an important way to understand them and inform the services and resources the library provides. In particular, we were interested in our students' study habits because of the important role they play in student success and library interactions.

There is little research about California community college students as a general population, apart from a 2006 Public Policy Institute of California report (Sengupta and Jepsen 2006). Existing research about the length of time college students study and how it relates to their academic performance does not look at particular study habits or focus on California community college students (Nonis and Hudson 2010). To learn more, we conducted a study to ask our students about their study habits, living situation, transportation options, work and family obligations, and methods of conducting research.

By gathering data directly from students and relying heavily on open-ended responses, the authors sought to better understand the needs of the students we serve.

INSTITUTIONAL CONTEXT

Coastline Community College and Modesto Junior College are both community colleges in California offering two-year degree programs and certificates. Coastline, in suburban Orange County, is unique in the California Community College system because a majority of its student population takes classes online. It has been suggested that "distance students are essentially commuter students who use a different vehicle to arrive on campuses" (Kretovics 2015, 73). For this reason, the library at Coastline has always been a 100 percent online or "Virtual Library." With the exception of a handful of dormitories for agricultural interns at Modesto, all of the students at both Coastline and Modesto are commuter students.

Coastline Community College and Modesto Junior College are located in different parts of the state and serve demographically distinct populations. Coastline is in coastal Orange County, which has a higher median income than the rest of the state. The population of the area has a slightly higher educational attainment level than the statewide average (U.S. Census Bureau 2016a). In contrast, Modesto is in California's Central Valley, which is one of the poorest parts of the state. Educational attainment levels there are also lower than the statewide average (U.S. Census Bureau 2016b).

TABLE 6.1

Institution statistics

FALL 2016	COASTLINE	MODESTO
Enrollment	9,718	17,707
Completion Rate	48.80%	43.00%
Distance Education	77.00%	17.00%
Students Age 24 or Younger	30.46%	65.82%
Ethnicity		
• African American	8.05%	3.36%
• Asian	24.19%	5.05%
• Hispanic	25.95%	49.76%
• White Non-Hispanic	29.39%	36.59%

SOURCE: California Community College Chancellor's Office. 2016. "Datamart."

According to the California Community College Chancellor's Datamart for Fall 2016, Modesto's enrollment was 17,707, nearly double the size of Coastline's 9,718, with students pursuing associate degrees, preparing for transfer to four-year institutions, or earning certificates. Student demographics at the two institutions are also different (table 6.1).

Modesto Junior College has two Library & Learning Centers, one on each of its two campuses, that provide traditional library services alongside tutoring support. Five full-time librarians, numerous support staff, and peer tutors serve thousands of students each week. Coastline has no physical library and serves predominantly distance-learning students. The "online library" is run by a single librarian with no support staff from any office at the college's administrative center or remotely. The library holds no print books or periodicals, and offers e-books and electronic journals, as well as text reference and online instruction and tutorials.

While Coastline and Modesto have significant differences in terms of their student demographics, physical library design, and focus on distance education and communities served, students at both colleges report remarkably similar experiences. As our survey results show, commuter students at California community colleges may be more alike than their outward differences might suggest.

Methods

In order to assess student study habits, we developed a survey instrument (Greene and Horan 2017) that included nineteen questions in four thematic sections: school, life, study habits, and research tools and technology. The survey was not intended to yield statistically significant data, but rather to provide some preliminary, comparable data about the study habits of the two student populations. The survey instrument used included both multiple choice and free response questions, none of which were required. This led to a different number of participants answering each question and, therefore, the quoted percentages throughout this chapter refer only to the number of responses to a given question.

To learn more broadly about student study habits, leading questions dealing with the library were intentionally avoided. Instead, open-ended and "select all that apply" options provided multiple ways to collect data about academic status and progress, living and work situation, research tools used for assignments, and specific study habits, such as where students study and why. Working with institutional research departments on each campus, the survey was administered to students at both colleges during a three-week period in February and March 2017. The survey instrument included a total of nineteen questions, with minor customizations for each college to address variations in terminology (e.g., the names of buildings and available resources).

At Coastline, the survey questions were added to the annual spring student survey and sent to all students who had taken a class during the previous three semesters. At Modesto, the Library & Learning Center administered the survey through the college's SurveyMonkey account and sent it to all students currently enrolled. In both cases, responses were collected anonymously and participants had the option to be entered into a raffle to win a $25 gift card. The Coastline survey had 1,030 responses while the Modesto survey had 558.

Data analysis was conducted in three ways once the survey was completed. The Coastline research office performed a data analysis for Coastline (Zentner, Covit, and Homestead 2017) and Modesto (Zentner and Greene 2017), producing a summary of the data. In addition, the authors' use of SurveyMonkey's text-analysis functionality helped show and support the categories found from the research office analysis. The authors also manually reviewed the data and reports in order to link smaller themes to bigger themes. The nature of the study did not require Institutional Review Board approval.

Survey Results

Modesto collected survey results a couple of weeks ahead of Coastline, and the authors were struck by the findings. Students were open and honest about their study habits, and some of their comments were eye-opening. When Coastline received the survey results, a side-by-side comparison of the data showed that the two student populations had similar study habits. In presenting the results, we have merged those from the school and life sections, since student responses showed how interwoven the two were. The remaining results are discussed for each of the two remaining survey sections: Study Habits and Research Tools and Technology.

School and Life

Survey respondents at both colleges were generally experienced college students and high achievers. A plurality of students at both colleges had completed seven or more semesters and sixty-one or more units, and were currently taking two or three classes. More than half of respondents at both colleges had 3.01 or higher grade point averages (GPAs), with most reporting GPAs higher than 3.51. One difference is that respondents at Coastline were far more likely to be taking a single course (35 percent) than at Modesto (12 percent), as illustrated by this student who conscientiously took fewer classes in order to manage her life and stress levels:

> I work part-time and go to school part-time so that I could spend time with family. To work full-time and go to school part-time on top of spending time with family and taking care of personal responsibilities is

only possible if I want to be under severe stress. I don't want to suffer from stress and lack of sleep, which is why I choose to work part-time and go to school part-time. —*Coastline student*

A strong majority of commuter students at both colleges lived at home with family and had a job. The percentage of working students was substantially higher than the nationwide average for full-time students, but lower than the average for part-time students (Perna 2010). The days of the week and the number of hours that students spent working were similar at both colleges during the week, but diverged on the weekends (figure 6.1). On Saturday and Sunday, Modesto's students reported working similar amounts to the rest of the week, while most Coastline students reported working one to four hours. This is perhaps a reflection of the higher percentage of Coastline students with a traditional Monday through Friday job.

The effort students put into coordinating work and school can be seen in the following quotes from the survey:

I try to put my school on one or two whole days and then work the rest of the week. I usually put work first because I need money. —*Coastline student*

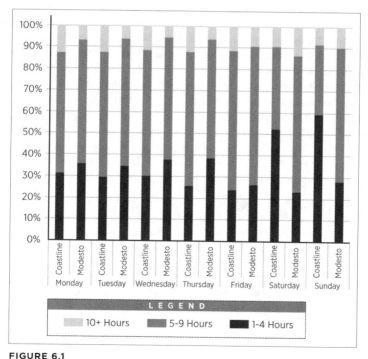

FIGURE 6.1

Hours spent working per day (Coastline *n* = 780, Modesto *n* = 316)

[I] have a part-time job as a substitute assistant teacher, and I only take the jobs that work with my schedule. —*Modesto student*

To the question, "If you multitask while studying, what kinds of activities do you do?" students responded with expected answers such as "listening to music" and "surf the Internet or social media," as well as some who adamantly stated they did not or could not multitask and study successfully. Open-ended responses provided snapshots into the very busy lives of commuter students at the community college. Since most students studied at home, many multi-tasked between home-related responsibilities and studying.

I might change a diaper or grab a snack but I don't tend to do anything else during my study periods. —*Modesto student*

I do laundry, wash dishes, cook, and straighten things up. I play videos tutorials on subjects I am learning while washing dishes, cooking, etc. Sometimes when I am cooking I study in the kitchen while I wait for things. I study while I wait for the laundry or wait in the car for my daughter or in the doctor's office lobby. Anywhere I am going to have to wait for something, I take something to study. —*Coastline student*

In response to the open-ended question, "How do you balance life, school and/or work commitments?" students at both colleges responded in similar ways. Time-management concepts such as scheduling time to study and using calendars were the most frequently reported approach for success (Coastline 33 percent, Modesto 38 percent). This aligns with earlier research that also found time management to be critical for students managing their hectic schedules (Stelnicki, Nordstokke, and Saklofske 2015). In addition, studies have shown that students who work are more likely to use time-management behaviors (Macan et al. 1990). Given that a majority of respondents on both campuses had jobs, high reliance on time-management techniques makes sense. Reviewing the responses individually revealed that technology tools such as calendar apps and reminders were heavily used to help manage time.

It's difficult, but I have learned time management is what has worked best. Prioritizing what [is] important now and what needs to be done and doing it in a timely manner. —*Coastline student*

I must stick to my routine and not get sidetracked. I go to work, come back home, do chores, put my children to sleep, then I start my home-work. I pull all-nighters sometimes and I put my schoolwork before even family time. My work is first to have food on the table, then education to provide a future, then my children/family. Without the first two I cannot be there for my family. I must be self-disciplined, focused, prioritize, and time manage. —*Modesto student*

Another group of responses identified through text analysis pertain to how challenging students found it to maintain a healthy balance between life, school, and work. A portion of respondents used words such as "difficult," "hard," or "barely" in their responses, suggesting that some students struggle with doing this successfully. Research has shown that commuter students not only deal with the typical stress of a student, but also have added stress from being a commuter student (Newbold 2015). Some of the coping methods mentioned in the research, such as task-focused adaptive measures as well as negative methods (e.g., avoidance), aligned with what students reported in our study habits survey. The challenges of maintaining a healthy balance was evident in many of the student responses, especially for parents of children, as can be seen in the following quotes:

> It is not going well, my job wants me to stop going to school or be fired. I also have an infant son, that I am the main caregiver [for]. —*Modesto student*

> It's hard. I'm a single Mom with a teenager. I work nights and homework is difficulty for me to do during the day so I study at night, but then I'm up late and tired in the morning. I'm trying to figure it out day to day. —*Coastline student*

Motivation to persist, focus, family support, and social sacrifices were also common themes in the responses, as illustrated in these quotes from the students about life, school, and work balance:

> I don't . . . I wish I could. I do really try, but sometimes it's really too much. If I try to catch up with my social life, I end up being behind on homework, even if it's just for one day (like today is my friend's birthday). If I spend time doing homework, I don't go out often. I probably go out once a week. —*Coastline student*

> I try to work efficiently. I put away my phone and try to focus on what I need to get done. This enables me to take short, refreshing breaks. Long-term, this is how I'm able to balance everything. —*Modesto student*

Keeping in mind that a strong majority of survey respondents at both colleges were high achievers, another similarity is that Coastline and Modesto students who use time-management techniques reported being more successful in college, a correlation long established in the literature (Macan et al. 1990). Our findings reaffirm that any focus on time-management skills by instructors and support services will benefit students.

Study Habits

The similarities between Coastline and Modesto commuter students was also apparent in the study habits section of the survey when students discussed hours, preferred locations for study, and frustrations. For example, the number of hours students studied each day were within ten percentage points of one another for every single benchmark (figure 6.2).

While research has shown that quality, not quantity of time spent studying is the key factor, the details of when and for how long students study is important for student and academic support services to know in order to align their hours as much as possible (Plant et al. 2005). Studying one to two hours per day was the most common response at both colleges every day of the week, and students studied more on Monday through Friday than on weekends. Notably, as the week progressed, more students at both colleges reported studying longer hours, but at the same time the number of students saying they did not study at all also increased. In fact, the highest number of "zero hours" spent studying was on Saturday at both colleges (Coastline 23 percent, Modesto 19 percent).

The survey asked where students studied and to select all that applied from a list of options that included traditional college spaces as well as spaces

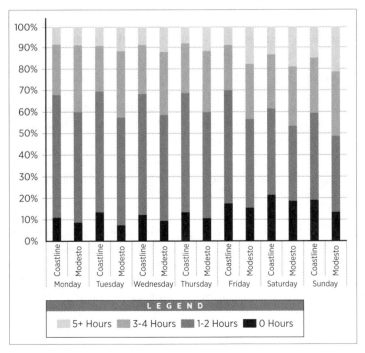

FIGURE 6.2

Hours spent studying per day (Coastline *n* = 1035, Modesto *n* = 445)

outside of a college setting. While roughly three-quarters of Coastline's students are distance learners, the number of Modesto students who studied at home was actually slightly higher (Coastline 92 percent, Modesto 94 percent). Unsurprisingly, Modesto students reported studying at home and on campus—including in the library—at higher rates than Coastline students. The overall results suggest that Modesto students did not study more; they simply studied in more places. Notably, some students report they studied at home despite regular distractions while others said the opposite, namely that studying at home helped them *avoid* distractions. These contradictory responses speak to both the diverse living situations that commuter students experience as well as their wide-ranging study environment preferences, as can be seen in the following quotes:

> My favorite place to study would have to be a peaceful location where I could focus. This usually happens to be my room. —*Coastline student*

> [My least favorite place to study is my] house due to the fact that there are endless distractions that pop up at all times. —*Modesto student*

In addition to studying at home, other locations that students from both colleges used to study included coffee shops, in a car, at a public library, outside, and at work. While some work environments are undoubtedly more conducive to studying than others, given that a large majority of the students we surveyed worked, finding employment that allowed for at least some time studying may well be an important factor in that student's likelihood of academic success.

> I look for a job that allows a flexible work schedule. I let my boss know well ahead of time that I'm a student. Everything else is just discipline. —*Coastline student*

> I'm able to do homework at work and I build my work schedule around school classes. —*Modesto student*

Locations where Coastline and Modesto showed more substantial study differences were related to traditional spaces on a college campus, with Modesto students more likely than Coastline students to indicate they studied in a college classroom before class and at the college's Library & Learning Centers. This could potentially be the result of Coastline having primarily online students and mini-campuses that are not actively used for studying.

These results have profound implications for supporting students' study habits. Nearly all of the common study locations were off campus, meaning that services will necessarily need to be effective at a distance. Institutions and libraries focused on distance education have been working on this problem for years, but even so, the scale of the situation may be underappreciated given that even face-to-face commuter students spend the vast majority of their study time off campus and at a distance from college resources.

When asked, "What is your favorite place to study and why?" many respondents said the library was their top choice because of the presence of other people focused on the same thing. One finding was that students at Coastline indicated the "library" was a favorite place to study, even though Coastline doesn't have a physical library. Further review of the data showed that Coastline students used the public library, libraries at neighboring colleges, and Coastline's student success centers, which they mistook for a Coastline library. Previous Coastline student surveys have shown that students identify the student success centers as the "library" at Coastline, potentially because these spaces are study spaces with computers, a textbook reserve library, and tutoring.

> [My favorite place to study is] in the school library because everyone around me is also studying. Plus I don't get very good reception in there so I am not constantly checking my phone. —*Modesto student*

> My favorite place to study would have to be at a coffee shop or the library. I choose these places because a coffee shop is typically quiet, and has snacks and drinks in case I'm there for most of the day and get hungry. The library is nice to study at too because not only is it quiet, but they have resources like books and computers if I need to use them. —*Coastline student*

Another common favorite location to study included "in a car" (Coastline 17 percent, Modesto 28 percent), which is a challenging space to study in even the best of circumstances. At the same time, some student comments revealed location-appropriate activities, such as listening to relevant audiobooks while driving. Some responses indicated students were multitasking while driving, while other responses suggested that students were parked and using the car as a study space, though the survey did not specify if studying was done while driving or sitting in a parked car.

> In the car. It's usually when I am driving. I listen to the audio software reading my textbook. I'm trying to be productive but it's often distracting because I'm multi-tasking while driving. —*Modesto student*

> [My favorite place to study is] my car/room. It's my personal space so I feel comfortable. —*Coastline student*

In summary, when asked about their favorite places to study, students were looking for a place that was quiet, comfortable, had Wi-Fi, and was free of distractions so they could concentrate. They also liked to be close to resources such as librarians, textbooks, computers, and study spaces. Many students mentioned food, yet many libraries, including Modesto's, continue to prohibit food in their facilities. In contrast, when asked about their least favorite place to study, students commonly talked about places with too much noise, too many distractions, and crowded spaces. That students crave quiet when

TABLE 6.2

Favorite places to study

	HOME (%)	LIBRARY (%)	COFFEE SHOP (%)
Coastline (*n* = 587)	65	12	10
Modesto (*n* = 393)	65	18	8

studying is well established in the literature, and contemporary library design practices intentionally take this into account (Howard 2012). Overall, students at Coastline and Modesto identified the same top three favorite places to study when the data was evaluated (table 6.2).

> My least favorite place to study is in a noisy environment because it prevents me from focusing on the task at hand. —*Coastline student*

Responses to the survey question about when students typically studied suggest that traditional library open/support hours may not be aligned with student study habits, as other studies have found (Foster and Gibbons 2007). When asked what time of day they typically studied, students at both colleges said the period from 8:00 P.M. to midnight was the most common study period (Coastline 55 percent, Modesto 65 percent). This is notable because many libraries, including Modesto's, are closed at this time. In addition, a substantial portion of students at both colleges reported studying from midnight to 4:00 A.M. Tutorials and research guides are available during these times, but there is no human assistance at either college. In fact, at the time, Modesto's proxy authentication was generally unavailable starting at midnight for several hours every day for maintenance.

> I try my best to do my online work once I'm done with home and family obligations. Which usually puts me at doing course work at 10 at night. And every once in a while I get it done earlier in the day. —*Coastline student*

> I have 2 children with my boyfriend. He works nights on an opposite schedule from my school schedule. I study when my children go to sleep so I stay up later. It's hard but sometimes you just have to suck it up and do what you have to do to get where you want to be in life. —*Modesto student*

The second most common study time was 4:00 P.M. to 8:00 P.M. (Coastline 44 percent, Modesto 51 percent), when face-to-face research requests decline as the evening approaches in the physical library at Modesto. Given some of the responses to the open-ended questions, this is likely because students are already home. Returning to campus would mean finding child care, leaving family, transportation time, and finding parking, all just to study in the library for one more hour. Coastline's library is virtual and potentially better suited to meet some of the needs of students studying when a traditional library is closed. Of note is that the Coastline librarian uses a Google Voice phone number for the library that rings the library office phone and also goes to the librarian's personal cell phone. This number can also be texted. Because of this, the Coastline librarian can answer library reference questions when a typical library would be closed. While not in high use, the librarian has been able to answer student questions during nontraditional times. The librarian has a little flexibility with scheduling and uses these reference opportunities as part of assigned virtual office hours.

Research Tools and Technology

In the final section of the survey, students were asked about the last research assignment they completed. The most common amount of time students at both colleges reported spending on their most recent assignment was between two and five hours (Coastline 61 percent, Modesto 53 percent). Follow-up questions asked about the types of tools and assistance that respondents used when conducting research. Continuing a trend, the answers were broadly similar at both colleges.

Students at both colleges said the most common technology they use to study were laptops (Coastline 80 percent, Modesto 84 percent) and smartphones (Coastline 53 percent, Modesto 74 percent). Desktop computers were the third most commonly selected technology at both colleges. When asked to "select all that apply" and shown a list of research tools, Google and Internet search ranked the highest followed by textbooks and Canvas, the learning management system (LMS) at both colleges. Notably, smartphone usage was one of the top four tools used to conduct research at both colleges (Coastline 22 percent, Modesto 41 percent).

The number of respondents saying they consulted a college librarian was lower at Coastline than Modesto, while a similar number of students at both colleges used a public librarian. This is perhaps not surprising given the different library configurations. Coastline is an entirely virtual library with a solo librarian, while Modesto has a physical library location on both of its two campuses and five full-time librarians. Research databases were less frequently cited by Coastline students than by Modesto students, and the generic "Library databases" option was chosen by 14 percent of Coastline students. These numbers did not match the substantial usage data for the Coastline library databases, but further evaluation showed that database vendor names are not associated with the databases on the library web page, and this might be something to consider in future surveys and library web design modifications. Meanwhile, Modesto students reported that they more frequently used EBSCO and Gale databases, while another 30 percent selected the generic "Library databases" option.

The final survey question asked who students turn to for help when conducting research. A plurality of students at both colleges didn't ask for help at all. Most students that did seek help at both colleges asked their instructor, classmate, family member, or friend for help. Librarians and tutors were used less frequently.

DISCUSSION AND LESSONS LEARNED

The authors were surprised at how alike the students at each institution were, based on their survey responses, especially in the School & Life section of the survey. This led to a revelation: in addition to being commuters, the students at Coastline and Modesto reported remarkably similar academic experiences, general living situations, work commitments, and approaches to finding a healthy work/school/life balance. There are some exceptions in the data, such as the number of hours spent working on weekends, but by and large the results are consistent despite the distinct student populations, local geography, and differing focus on distance education at Coastline and Modesto.

Of interest in the survey data was that the most common study spaces were off campus. This is directly related to students being commuters versus living on campus. Students identified looking for study spaces that are quiet, comfortable, have Wi-Fi, and are free of distractions so they could concentrate. They also liked to be close to food and resources. Some students report liking light background noise, such as at a coffee shop.

The authors took the responses from the most favorite and least favorite places to study questions and discussed what an ideal library space might look like. The results suggest that students want different types of spaces, but can small libraries be more than one space? With many community college libraries in California undergoing renovations or being added to new buildings with local bond measure funding, library space is an ongoing topic of discussion. Based on student comments, the authors came up with a space designed to best serve commuter students, although it might also appeal more broadly to other academic situations. An ideal library space would include three distinct but connected areas: (1) a quiet zone with no computers, group work, or phones allowed; (2) a calm study space, with light background music, like a coffee shop; and (3) a noisier space with peer tutoring. Librarians and other support staff would be at a hub that is easily accessible to all three areas. These spaces would have numerous noise-proof study rooms and would include a cafe attached to all three areas.

Building or even redesigning a library space is impractical for most libraries, but there are other, more practical ways to address commuter students' needs for study space. Specifically, the authors discussed identifying and marketing quiet places to study on campus and, for Coastline especially, in the community, and providing that information on the library website. Another concept the authors revisited was food in the library. Based on the number of students who indicated their favorite place to study was close to food, it seems appropriate that libraries should review food policies if they are trying to create inviting study spaces.

While the library ranked in the top four favorite places to study at both colleges, the majority of studying was reported to be done off campus and during hours the library was not open, specifically at home in the late evening. The mismatch between library hours and student study habits is challenging to resolve. The authors believe that the solution is not longer library hours, an approach sometimes taken, especially at residential institutions (Albanese 2005). Previous experience and reference statistics have shown that face-to-face library assistance is not frequently sought later in the evening. Instead, these findings create an opportunity for colleges with traditional libraries to think of how they also have a virtual library of their own. All students become distance students when they leave campus. Current students expect to interact with a college and its services online (Kretovics 2015); it is each library's responsibility to continuously improve this interaction. Library websites are a portal for hundreds of resources and could potentially be redesigned to better serve students when the physical library is closed. A few ways to accomplish this include reviewing website navigation and naming structures to make sure they are clear to students; improving the quality for resources by curating based on quality, not quantity; and ensuring that instructions for users are clear and concise, especially for off-campus authentication. A marketing campaign to highlight the "Library After-Hours" could showcase library resources that are available 24/7.

At Coastline and Modesto, the library website and other resources are always being modified to better serve distance students. Another way to have library resources available to distance students is to embed them in the LMS (Daniels and Usina 2016). Having library resources inside the LMS is one way to provide access to the library for students regardless of their physical location. The library at Coastline is in the process of embedding library resources in the Canvas LMS, and it assumes that the majority of the student population will be accessing library resources after normal business hours. For this reason, lots of how-to videos are being created as well as step-by-step tutorials. The faculty at Coastline have always known there was only a virtual library, and this has helped market the library's resources to students via the website.

In the Research Tools and Technology section, commuter students reported using textbooks and smartphones for research assignments much more than the authors anticipated, which opened up a conversation about what those responses mean for the library. It underscores the importance of having textbooks available for students to use, since students ranked them as one of the most-used tools in this survey. Yet libraries typically put textbooks in reserve collections with limited circulation parameters, such as two-hour loan periods and library use only restrictions. This may be a policy worth reconsidering, given that our commuter students most commonly report studying in the evening after many libraries close. Making more textbooks available overnight would better align textbook availability with student study habits.

The high smartphone usage reported for research was notable to the authors despite the surge in their popularity over the past decade. When asked what percentage of research was conducted on a smartphone during the last research project they completed, usage was widespread. Roughly three-quarters of students used their smartphone at least some amount. However, roughly half of students reported using their smartphone for a relatively small percentage (less than 25 percent) of their research, while much lower numbers used it for more than half of their research. Still, these results highlight the importance of smartphones in students' research practices and led to an outcome for both Coastline and Modesto to find more effective ways to help students conduct research on their smartphones. Smartphone-specific tutorials and specific library instruction focused on mobile environments might better prepare students to work with library resources as they are likely to do in practice. At the same time, librarians need to continue working with database vendors to advocate for more mobile-friendly products.

The study habits survey provided the authors with substantial data and spearheaded discussion and next steps at both colleges. It also provided some lessons learned for the authors, most notably related to survey design and implementation. The authors created the survey, tested it, and solicited feedback from multiple sources prior to releasing it. Still, when the results came in, the authors realized they had made some mistakes. For instance, there were a few items that were hard to compare because the answer options had been set up in slightly different ways at the two colleges. One example is related to the number of hours that students work and study. Coastline had set up the answers as a range, while Modesto allowed students to select single numbers. Another problem was the way Modesto's question on students' living situation was configured within SurveyMonkey. Respondents were able to select more than one answer option (e.g., alone and simultaneously with two roommates), leading to some conflicting submissions. In contrast, Coastline's survey used skip logic to separate responses into separate pages, which captured the data more accurately. Lastly, while the open-ended questions elicited the most compelling data, they proved time-consuming and challenging to analyze and compare the data between the two colleges. In the future, if questions are being compared across colleges, there should be a discussion about reducing the number of open-ended questions if coding is a priority for data analysis. The open-ended questions did provide valuable data, so it would be best if they could be kept and a cleaner data analysis model was used to compare data.

CONCLUSIONS

The results of the survey of student study habits stimulated an engaging conversation between the authors that then spread out to each college campus. While initially the idea was to see where the library intersects with student study habits, the results prompted the authors to reimagine how the library could best support students when they study regardless of where they are physically located. Eliminating barriers to access is a foundational goal for both libraries and community colleges. Yet the results prompted a discussion that went beyond improving access. The authors discussed the idea of making the library easy for students to use and access, including the physical space as well as the online resources.

After looking at the technology that our commuter students reported using to study, it became apparent that the authors' libraries need to better support students who are conducting research with a smartphone. At the same time, given that a majority of students reported using Google for their research, does it make sense to link library databases to Google Scholar and train students how to use that since they are already familiar with the Google interface? It would be interesting to see if community colleges with discovery services have more students reporting using the library for research as opposed to using Google. Additionally, in future surveys, would it make sense to ask students what *kind* of research they are doing on their smartphones? It is possible the authors are making assumptions about what students consider "research."

The authors agree that in the future they would like to survey students about their study habits at least once a year. Coastline has committed to surveying students each fall in order to inform study space design at the college and services to students at a distance. In addition, since the study ended, author Greene accepted a new position at Columbia College (the sister college to Modesto) and hopes to find support to survey students there about their study habits. Both authors are curious to see if the students at Columbia, also a community college in California, will have similar results to students at Coastline and Modesto. If two seemingly dissimilar colleges such as Coastline and Modesto report similar results, it warrants asking if other California community colleges would also yield similar results. The authors have reached out to the statewide Council of Chief Librarians about bringing the survey to all 114 California community colleges in the coming year. The authors found the survey results to be very informative, and think fellow librarians would, too.

REFERENCES

Albanese, Andrew Richard. 2005. "The Best Thing a Library Can Be Is Open" *Library Journal* 130 (15): 42–45. http://lj.libraryjournal.com/2005/09/managing -libraries/the-best-thing-a-library-can-be-is-open/.

Badger, Caitlin W. 2014. "A Student Perspective: Commuter Student Experiences, Definitions and Self-Identification." *Humphrey Public Affairs Review*. http:// humphreyreview.umn.edu/student-perspective-commuter-student-experiences -definitions-and-self-identification.

Daniels, Erin, and Phyllis Usina. 2016. "Creating a Library Presence in Canvas." California Community Colleges. http://ccconlineed.org/wp-content/uploads/ 2017/02/Creating-a-Library-Presence-in-Canvas-CCL-10–28–16-A11Y.pdf.

"Datamart." 2016. California Community Colleges Chancellor's Office. http:// datamart.cccco.edu/datamart.aspx.

Foster, Nancy Fried, and Susan L. Gibbons, eds. 2007. *Studying Students: The Undergraduate Research Project at the University of Rochester*. Chicago: Association of College & Research Libraries.

Greene, Brian, and Elizabeth Horan. 2017. "Study Habits of Community College Students." Survey. https://drive.google.com/file/d/0B61601dJZKYBTXE xc3FHYTd6clk/view.

Howard, Jennifer. 2012. "At Libraries, Quiet Makes a Comeback." *Chronicle of Higher Education*, July 20. www.chronicle.com/article/At-Libraries-Quiet-Makes-a/ 132885.

Kretovics, Mark. 2015. "Commuter Students, Online Services, and Online Communities." *New Directions for Student Services* 2015 (150): 69–78. doi:10 .1002/ss.20128.

Macan, Therese H., Comila Shahani, Robert L. Dipboye, and Amanda P. Phillips. 1990. "College Students' Time Management: Correlations with Academic Performance and Stress." *Journal of Educational Psychology* 82 (4): 760–68. doi:10.1037/0022 –0663.82.4.760.

Newbold, John J. 2015. "Lifestyle Challenges for Commuter Students." *New Directions for Student Services* 2015 (150): 79–86. doi:10.1002/ss.20129.

Nonis, Sarath A., and Gail I. Hudson. 2010. "Performance of College Students: Impact of Study Time and Study Habits." *Journal of Education for Business* 85 (4): 229–38. doi:10.1080/08832320903449550.

Perna, Laura W. 2010. *Understanding the Working College Student: New Research and Its Implications for Policy and Practice*. Sterling, VA: Stylus Publishing.

Plant, E. Ashby, K. Anders Ericsson, Len Hill, and Kia Asberg. 2005. "Why Study Time Does Not Predict Grade Point Average across College Students: Implications of Deliberate Practice for Academic Performance." *Contemporary Educational Psychology* 30 (1): 96–116. doi:10.1016/j.cedpsych.2004.06.001.

Sengupta, Ria, and Christopher Jepsen. 2006. "California's Community College Students." *California Counts: Population Trends and Profiles* 8 (2): 1–24. www.ppic .org/publication/californias-community-college-students/.

Stelnicki, Andrea M., David W. Nordstokke, and Donald H. Saklofske. 2015. "Who Is the Successful University Student? An Analysis of Personal Resources." *Canadian*

Journal of Higher Education 45 (2): 214–28. http://files.eric.ed.gov/fulltext/EJ1073616.pdf.

U.S. Census Bureau. 2016a. "Table DP03—Selected Economic Characteristics." 2011–2015 American Community Survey 5-Year Estimates. https://factfinder.census.gov.

———. 2016b. "Table S1501—Educational Attainment." 2011–2015 American Community Survey 5-Year Estimates. https://factfinder.census.gov.

Zentner, Aeron, and Brian Greene. 2017. "Modesto Student Study Habits." Modesto Junior College. http://libguides.mjc.edu/ld.php?content_id=32782626.

Zentner, Aeron, Raissa Covit, and Steven Homestead. 2017. "Coastline Student Study Habits." Coastline Community College. http://documents.coastline.edu/research%20and%20planning/Research/Research%20Studies/2017%20Student%20Study%20Habits.pdf.

TANNER WRAY and
NANCY FRIED FOSTER

7

Making the Library Work for Community College Commuters

The Case of Montgomery College

I f you provide a "generic" academic library at a community college, will it meet students' needs? Probably not, according to research conducted on three community college campuses in Montgomery County, Maryland. Providing the most effective libraries to these students requires a new understanding of who they are and how they conduct their academic work. Community college students, who are overwhelmingly commuters, need a library oriented more to teaching and learning than to research. Because they are older on average than four-year college students, community college students are more likely to have families and jobs that take them away from campus. Their programs are more diverse, ranging from honors academic programs to vocational programs to developmental English and math classes. These differences affect academic work practices and campus use patterns, leading to distinctive needs for library resources, spaces, services, and technology. In the following pages, we discuss how one nonresidential community college system engaged over 1,400 members of the college community in a project to improve the library in an informed way. After a discussion of the project's aims and questions, we describe Montgomery College and provide an overview of our methods and findings. We conclude by showing that the information we gained, combined with the project's inclusive approach, enabled specific improvements to be made to the library while increasing the library's ability to identify and respond to the needs of its large commuter undergraduate community.

THE RESEARCH QUESTION

The ethnographic project was launched at Montgomery College Libraries with a primary objective of gaining a better understanding of how the libraries were used and what changes in the libraries might help students do their academic work and take better advantage of their academic opportunities. Another objective was to provide students with real-life opportunities for research and design.

The project followed the general framework and process of a previous project at the University of Maryland, which included studies that library employees conducted using ethnographic methods, additional ethnographic studies by graduate anthropology students, and design work by graduate architecture students (Steele et al. 2015). Although there are no graduate students at Montgomery College—indeed, there are only freshmen and sophomores in the college degree programs—all components of the original study were included, albeit on an adjusted scale. Additionally, the Montgomery College project asked stakeholders on all three of the college's campuses to provide guidance to the project, help disseminate findings, and reinforce outcomes. Stakeholder groups included representatives from major administrative and operational units as well as librarians and members of the academic staff. Over 1,400 members of the Montgomery College community participated, including students, faculty members, staff, and administrators, making the project very broad and inclusive and providing numerous opportunities for students to become involved, whether as researchers, respondents, or designers.[1]

With regard to the project's primary objective, to gain a better understanding of how the library was used and what changes might benefit students, the research question was stated broadly but the methods were designed to capture a great deal of detail. Project leaders wanted to know who was in the library and what activities they were conducting, including some specifics of their work practices; why they sat where they did; whether they worked alone or with others; what helped and hindered their work; what they read and how they learned of it, acquired it, and read it; and where they conducted academic work if not in the library.

Alongside the library-led project and under their professors' direction, students in anthropology classes also conducted ethnographic research. The students had five research questions to address: How do students and faculty typically use the Montgomery College Libraries? What are the needs and expectations of students and faculty when using a library? Are there aspects of library services and programs that might work better if improved or modified? How do students and faculty feel about working in and enjoying the library space? Are there aspects of the library space (visual, spatial, auditory) that could be improved to support better concentration, comfort, and aesthetic appreciation for library users?

It is important to note that the project tilted in the direction of design research. While the researchers sought basic information about student practices and needs, the studies were oriented toward practical outcomes, that is, identifying ways to improve the library system's spaces, services, and resources. This was motivated by a desire to better support students, since it was believed that a greater understanding of how and where students did well or struggled in their work would provide an informational basis upon which to develop design concepts. At the same time, the project's design was matched to the mission and resources of the library and to the teaching and learning needs of faculty and student participants. For this reason, it was appropriate to conduct limited studies oriented to library use and improvement rather than full-blown ethnographic research. The studies conducted by anthropology students both supported the overall objectives of the project and accomplished specific course-related teaching and learning work.[2]

MONTGOMERY COLLEGE

Montgomery College, the community college of Montgomery County, Maryland, provides approximately 34,400 credit students and 56,000 students overall with a variety of programs in general education, career preparation, workforce development, and continuing education. The student body is diverse in background with no majority race, nearly 6,500 non-U.S. citizens, and 159 foreign countries represented. The college has three campuses, two additional sites dedicated to workforce development and continuing education, and two community engagement centers. Montgomery College is a nonresidential institution and all students are commuters. Montgomery College's mission statement says: "We empower our students to change their lives, and we enrich the life of our community. We are accountable for our results." All faculty and employees share a commitment to this mission and to student success.

No two students are alike—except in their role as commuters. Student goals are diverse, with some students preparing for transfer into four-year bachelor's degree programs, others preparing for a career change or the job market, and still others engaging in lifelong learning. Some have the personal and family resources to succeed, but others face a range of financial, linguistic, and societal obstacles. Many are the first in their families to attend college, and lack family models for succeeding academically. The college has many students who are recent immigrants who may still be learning English, veterans returned from military service overseas, and men and women holding down one or more jobs while developing the skills for better employment. Many have responsibility for their own children or for other family members. As a result, Montgomery College students follow many different pathways through the education system. The complexity of their lives has a direct bearing on how the library needs to position itself to support them and help them meet their goals.

In support of the mission and the institutional focus on student success, Montgomery College provides four libraries on its three campuses. The Rockville and Germantown campuses both have general libraries, while the Takoma Park/Silver Spring campus has both a general and an art library. The Montgomery College Libraries employ 22 librarians and 26 staff plus student employees across the four facilities to support teaching and learning as well as student and institutional research, and to deliver electronic and physical resources to the Montgomery College community. Overall, the libraries provide access to over 200,000 printed books and 145 electronic databases and related resources, as well as approximately 98,000 e-journals, 60,000 e-books, and 75,000 streaming videos.

In addition to electronic and physical resources, the libraries provide a number of services to support student and faculty success. Librarians provide group instruction sessions and personal research consultations. Users can obtain research assistance in person or they can get help online through the 24/7 AskUsNow librarian chat service or the libraries' online subject and course guides. The libraries provide a variety of study environments to fit all learning preferences, including private group study rooms and collaboration areas. The libraries provide computer workstations and an in-library laptop and tablet loaning service. Additional technology services include high-speed scanners, video production equipment, and collaborative workstations for group projects.

METHODS

Montgomery College's libraries coordinated the overall project comprising studies conducted by library teams and anthropology classes, as well as design work done by architecture students. Library teams and anthropology students conducted studies on all three campuses over the three years of the project, including the Rockville campus in the first year (2013/14), the Takoma Park/Silver Spring campus in the second year (2014/15), and the Germantown campus in the final year (2015/16). Architecture students were engaged on the Rockville campus in the first year of the project.

Participatory Design Activities by Library Teams

Research and stakeholder activities conducted by library teams over the three years of the project included 911 students, 56 faculty members, 42 library employees, 19 administrators, and 41 other college employees. The library teams' studies had two significant characteristics. They gathered extensive, actionable information upon which to base library improvements. Equally importantly, the project brought together people in widely varying roles from many units across the college's three main campuses to conduct the studies, reflect on the findings, and envision change.

The particular approach taken in this project was participatory design, a departure from traditional design processes that rely more heavily on precedent, that is, on the expertise of previous designers. The participatory design process engages a broader range of experts to understand and describe current and emerging work practices, identify unmet needs, and develop solutions to those needs. To conduct a participatory design process, a facilitator, supported by a project team, creates structured opportunities for students, employees, and other nontraditional experts to provide information about how they do their work and how it might go better. This is done through the use of such activities as interviews, observations, and the creation of photos, drawings, and other artifacts that provide a framework for conversations about work practices and preferences. The final step is to interpret the information provided in the course of these activities, develop qualitative requirements, and make design recommendations.

Participatory design intentionally considers the whole community as equal stakeholders in a design process, albeit with different forms of expertise and complementary or even divergent interests. This approach was a particularly apt choice because it engaged the commuting students as both researchers and respondents in studying their own nonresidential campuses. Moreover, Montgomery College accomplished this on a fairly large scale with a modest investment and significant rewards.

Participatory or user-centered approaches have been used extensively in library technology and space design, especially since the 2005 publication of a study of faculty use of preprints, unpublished reports, and other grey literature in connection with the design of the institutional repository at the University of Rochester (Foster and Gibbons 2005). That study demonstrated the value of understanding academic work practices before identifying requirements for software development in academic libraries. The additional benefits of participatory design—the increased connection and engagement among librarians and academics—were described two years later with regard to a study of undergraduate work practices at the University of Rochester (Anderson and Marshall 2007). Both benefits were explicitly sought in the Montgomery College project, that is, the assessment was designed to develop information and collaboration at the same time.

Project leaders recruited library teams in successive years on the three campuses to conduct research activities and help analyze and interpret results. Each team included librarians and library staff as well as representatives from other college units: Grants and Sponsored Programs on one campus, and

Writing, Reading, and Language Centers on two campuses. The non-library members increased the size of the team and how much research they could conduct, and provided helpful, semi-outsider perspectives.

The campus-based teams ran a short survey within the library (reply cards) and engaged students in brief interviews at non-library campus locations (spot interviews). Additionally, at Rockville and Takoma Park/Silver Spring, the team conducted charrettes (design workshops) with faculty members, library employees, and students. These methods were selected to provide a picture of student library use, including work practices related to completing assignments, studying, and doing project work, as well as faculty and staff needs related to the library.

The reply cards were handed out in several areas in each of the four libraries and included questions about what respondents were doing, why they were in their chosen locations, and where they would go if forced to go elsewhere. The cards also asked for basic demographic information.

The spot interviews were conducted with students who were intercepted at non-library campus locations. By recruiting and interviewing students outside of the library, the project was able to include diverse students, both library users and non-users, in a wide range of programs. In these interviews, students were asked where they had last done work for a class outside of class time, why they had selected that location, how their work had gone, and what would have helped the work go better. They were also asked about their most recent non-textbook reading for a class.

The design workshops held on two of the campuses (Rockville and Takoma Park/Silver Spring) included students, faculty members, and employees of the libraries as participants. The participants created drawings of ideal library spaces and were then asked to talk about what they imagined themselves and others doing in the spaces. As with the other methods, the focus in the design workshops was on the activities in which people were engaged, or hoped to engage, in the library or with library services, resources, or technologies.

Each year, the campus-based library team analyzed and interpreted the data with the help of the consulting anthropologist. Data analysis began with the construction of Excel spreadsheets into which verbatim responses were transcribed. These verbatim responses were examined and discussed iteratively to develop codes, which were then inserted into the spreadsheets. Basic statistics revealed trends in activity, duration, and location of study, individual and group work, reasons for selecting study location, and so on. The pivot table feature of Excel made it possible to identify some interactions among the variables.[3]

Ethnographic Studies by Anthropology Students

In addition to the studies conducted by the library teams, students in anthropology classes conducted observations and interviews to understand current use of the libraries, student and faculty needs and expectations, and whether any changes to library services and facilities could improve concentration, comfort, and outcomes. Over three years, 290 anthropology student researchers participated in the project, including students from twelve ANTH 201 (Introduction to Sociocultural Anthropology) classes, ANTH 201 students from the Montgomery Scholars Honors Program and Honors Module, and students from the college's Renaissance Scholars Program.

The students were taught how to conduct structured interviews and in-library observations, and through these activities they interviewed 306 fellow students and 23 faculty members. Eight members of the college's full-time anthropology faculty developed the interview and observation forms, associated classroom assignments, and methods for analysis and modeling. Three part-time faculty members and an honors faculty member supported implementation on all three campuses.

Students conducted structured interviews in non-library campus locations. Two researchers were present at each interview, one in the role of interviewer and the other taking notes on the responses. Respondents included students from the general student population as well as faculty and students in smaller groups representing selected campus communities. These groups included general full-time and part-time faculty, students who had accommodations with Disability Support Services, students in the American English Language Program, evening students, and students who were military veterans. Nursing students, nursing faculty, and arts faculty were interviewed on the Takoma Park/Silver Spring campus to understand how their needs were being met by the two campus libraries that were some distance from each other.

Students conducted observations in the four campus libraries during morning, afternoon, and evening sessions. In thirty-minute periods, student observers either noted entrances, exits, and general activities in the space or coded specific activities in selected areas.

Each year, the student teams analyzed and interpreted the data with the help of their faculty. Data analysis began with the construction of Excel spreadsheets into which verbatim responses and observational data were entered. Groups of students reviewed the data to determine underlying themes, which they then used to develop concept models, findings, and recommendations.

Design Work by Architecture Students

Students in an architecture class participated in the project by developing design concepts for the library on the Rockville campus based on findings from the studies conducted by library teams and anthropology students. A member of Montgomery College's full-time architecture faculty led the students and provided them with the following functional goals for a redesign of the library:

- A welcoming space that is easy to navigate
- A space that helps students feel welcome, secure, comfortable, and able to do serious work
- A variety of spaces including group study and quiet areas
- A unified service desk

The ARCH 201 (Introduction to Architectural Design) course covered the spectrum of architectural design, including programming, sustainable strategies, structural logic, envelope design, space planning, environmental influence, and aesthetics. The centerpiece of the course was the library project, in which students were asked to draw from the ethnographic studies as well as facilities information provided by Central Facilities. The twenty-one students in the class worked in four teams to develop four potential futures for the Rockville campus library. At the end of the semester, the teams presented their ideas to a jury that included architecture faculty from the college, architects from architectural firms, and the library director.

RESULTS

Library teams and anthropology classes not only collected but also analyzed and interpreted the data independently. The two sets of findings were then integrated to support planning and decision-making, as described below.

Findings from Participatory Design Activities Conducted by Library Teams

The campus-based library teams analyzed and interpreted the data and learned, first of all, that there were some differences but also marked similarities across the three campuses.

On all three campuses of this community college, the library provides a special place for students in which they can give their attention to their studies without distraction. For some students, there are few alternatives. Montgomery College students, like those at other community colleges, tend to be older than students at the four-year colleges that are better documented in the ethnographic literature. Many of them have jobs and family responsibilities that leave little time for studying; they appear to make careful use of their time on campus, taking advantage of even short stretches of study time when they can.

Students who come to the library are drawn by the things that contribute to an atmosphere of quiet concentration and focus. This includes everything from suitable furnishings to adequate power and good Wi-Fi, as well as noise dampening and soothing décor. Students want to feel welcome and secure. Most reported that they worked alone. While many students reported sitting next to other students, they did not necessarily know these other people. Respondents did not consider commercial establishments, such as coffee shops, to be good alternatives to the library.

Students make extensive use of online information resources, but they do not limit their use of these resources to time spent in the library. Only a small number of the students responding to reply cards distributed within the library were using library-supplied resources at the time. Reading, in particular, is an activity that most responding students reported doing at home. Furthermore, these students show a marked preference for reading on a screen.

The range of reading materials that respondents reported using is quite broad. Not all students at Montgomery College read academic books and articles, and many of the respondents who do so read material recommended and even provided by their professors or instructors. Unlike the four-year colleges that are better represented in the literature, all three campuses of this community college offer a wide range of workforce training programs in addition to academic courses. A small but significant number of the students who responded to on-campus interviews had not yet read a book or an article for any class; several had only read from the assigned textbook. Others read job-related explanatory material, such as charts and posters, or magazine articles and other popular reading material.

Findings from Ethnographic Studies Done by Anthropology Students

The anthropology students' ethnographic studies indicated that while each library facility is quite different, responding to its own set of very specific needs, there were common themes across the three campuses.

The studies showed that students need greater access to technology and especially to computers and electrical outlets. The studies also found that students make little use of tutorials, course pages, and other online resources and may not fully understand the availability and value of course reserve materials. According to the ethnographic studies conducted in the anthropology courses, many students are reluctant to ask library employees to assist them, thereby missing an available source of help.

The students' ethnographic studies also discovered that respondents found fault with library facilities. They wanted more comfortable seating and a greater variety of work spaces and would like to add more artwork and more colorful surroundings. Respondents also found some areas of the library to be congested and lighting was identified as a problem, with respondents saying that some library areas were noticeably dim.

OUTCOMES

Repeatedly over the three years of the project, the library emerged for students as an excellent space in which to devote themselves to their studies away from the demands and distractions of jobs and family. For commuter students at community colleges, minutes and hours spent in the library can be essential to achieving their education goals.

The information gathered during the study provided a rich source of information for strategic planning and the identification of short-, medium-, and long-range library improvements. In each year of the project, the library team developed a list of possible implementations that were considered by a campus-based implementation team in light of additional information sources such as the 2014 LibQUAL+ survey results and institution-wide planning documents. Each implementation team selected, refined, and added to the concepts and then initiated the work of putting these ideas into practice. Some of these concepts, such as a need for more outlets, related to basic infrastructure, but many more related to designing spaces that enable students to work with standard technologies, get help when needed, use the many resources the libraries provide at no cost, feel inspired, and focus on the work at hand rather than their many other cares. Because the ethnographic data were integrated with institutional information, implementations have aligned with the college's strategic directions.

In developing and implementing concepts, the libraries were keen to address the documented needs of the real people who participated in the studies. Some changes were instituted across the libraries because they address universal conditions and needs of Montgomery College students.

Extended Open Hours

Because so many commuting students lack access to good study environments outside of campus, the libraries piloted extended evening hours, from 8:00 P.M. to 10:00 P.M., Monday through Wednesday. After collecting and analyzing additional behavior-mapping data during those hours, the schedule change was extended to Thursday and made permanent.

Technology Upgrades

Commuter students may not own the technology they need to complete their schoolwork, or it may be difficult for them to carry it to campus. The libraries upgraded technology based on users' highest priorities, circulating laptops and tablets within the libraries, providing high-speed scanners, and offering easy-to-use video recording studios, known as One Button Studios, that do not require any prior video production experience. Technology use is monitored to ensure that offerings are meeting needs. Discussions are underway about other ways that the libraries can support the technology needs of students.

More Electrical Outlets

When commuter students bring their devices with them, they need to keep them charged. Additional power outlets, including USB outlets, have been installed in all libraries, increasing public outlets by 67 percent. Charging stations were also added.

Easier Access to E-Resources

Commuter students may not have time to come to the library to access content housed in tangible form, such as books and journals. Access to e-resources was improved with implementation of a discovery services system, expanded e-resource collections, and better service promotion. All students can access the content regardless of time of day and location.

Improved Web Services and Communication

The navigation of online content and effective communications from the library were found to be so important to the success of commuter students that the libraries created a new position to address these issues. The new web services and communications librarian leads a communications committee, also recently created, to increase awareness of the Montgomery College Libraries, improve understanding and competence, and increase use of the libraries' resources, services, and initiatives by members of the Montgomery College and Montgomery County communities.

A More Inspiring Library Environment

The homes of commuter students may not provide space that allows them to do their best work. In many cases, it falls to the library to provide spaces that inspire and motivate commuter students. The libraries have been adding new furniture that is mobile and more comfortable, installing more artwork, repainting walls, and installing new carpeting in their facilities.

More Spaces for Quiet Work and Group Work

Commuter students may only see their classmates on campus, and libraries are well placed to support their desire for group work spaces in addition to the quiet and silent zones that so many of them need. The libraries are working to establish zoning in the libraries to ensure adequate quiet areas and are working to increase the number of group study rooms.

More Accessible Help

Commuter students need libraries that are easy to navigate and in which they can easily find the expertise they seek. Accordingly, the libraries are planning to implement single service desks. These desks will ultimately be staffed principally by access services employees, who will manage the library facilities and services. Librarians will be increasingly deployed both virtually and physically to student locations, including classrooms and the learning management system.

More Textbooks and Open Educational Resources

Commuter students may not have the resources to purchase textbooks or may not want to carry books with them. The libraries have purchased textbooks to expand and improve the textbook course reserve program. The libraries are also supporting the college's open educational resources initiative to improve college affordability.

Designing the Future

In addition to the implementations that are already underway, the libraries have plans for future changes. To provide even better support to commuter students, the libraries have worked with an architect on conceptual designs for short-term and long-term facilities changes. The priorities and themes of those changes are informed by the ethnographic work and include:

- Reconfiguring the three larger libraries so that the highest-profile services (service desk, technology, instruction and group rooms) are available on the main floor
- Increasing technology hubs and offerings
- Establishing or formalizing defined study areas based on observed student work practices and preferences
- Increasing the number of group study rooms
- Diversifying the types of work spaces offered to students
- Reducing print collections and reconfiguring book stacks to free up space for other uses
- Developing effective monitoring and outreach within the libraries to identify and respond more quickly to patron needs

- Improving consultation areas in which library employees can work with students

In addition to the more visible changes listed above, the libraries are implementing several behind-the-scenes changes, including:

- Realigning the staffing structure to better support the initiatives described here
- Redefining library jobs and enhancing employee skills as needed
- Increasing the use of student employees to provide peer-to-peer services
- Partnering with the college to provide online and embedded in-person support services to students
- Assuring a strong relationship with Safety and Security to maintain safety

CONCLUSION

The main purpose of the Montgomery College ethnographic studies was to discover how the college's students accomplish their academic work and what they need and prefer in twenty-first-century library spaces, services, and programs. With that understanding, the Montgomery College Libraries are actively working to implement changes based on what was learned while identifying further information needs that may drive future studies.

The structure and scope of the project resulted in much more than a mere understanding of what library users need to succeed at Montgomery College and a road map for changes. The project produced a stronger institution-wide understanding of student needs and the role the libraries fill in supporting student success. Through the research and design courses offered to students, the libraries established themselves in a new role, as research leaders and partners, and as a lab for students to experience real-life learning, original research, and design. Through the project, students in the anthropology, honors, Scholars, and architecture programs learned their craft and developed presentation skills. Honors program students presented a panel on the study at a regional honors conference. Other students made presentations to college-wide stakeholder groups, library teams, and award juries.

The impact was not just on college students and stakeholders. Montgomery College Libraries employees learned valuable new skills and engaged with our students differently. Methods learned in the studies are being utilized on a smaller scale to inform additional changes. Strong and enduring partnerships have been forged in the project and will serve the college's students, the Montgomery College Libraries, and the college well into the future.

REFERENCES

Anderson, Helen, and Ann Marshall. 2007. "What an Experience: Library Staff Participation in Ethnographic Research." In *Studying Students: The Undergraduate Research Project at the University of Rochester,* edited by Nancy Fried Foster and Susan Gibbons, 55–62. Chicago: Association of College & Research Libraries.

Foster, Nancy Fried, and Susan Gibbons. 2005. "Understanding Faculty to Improve Content Recruitment for Institutional Repositories." *D-Lib Magazine* 11 (1). www.dlib.org/dlib/january05/foster/01foster.html.

Steele, Patricia A., David Cronrath, Sandra Parsons Vicchio, and Nancy Fried Foster. 2015. *The Living Library: An Intellectual Ecosystem.* Chicago: Association of College & Research Libraries.

Wray, Tanner, Cynthia Pfanstiehl, and Nancy Fried Foster. 2017. "Collaborative Libraries Assessment across a Multi-Campus College." In *Proceedings of the 2016 Library Assessment Conference: Building Effective, Sustainable, Practical Assessment, October 31–November 2, 2016, Arlington, VA,* edited by Sue Baughman, Steve Hiller, Katie Monroe, and Angela Pappalardo, 259–64. Washington, DC: Association of Research Libraries. http://libraryassessment.org/archive/conference-proceedings-2016.shtml.

NOTES

1. For more information about project participants, see Wray, Pfanstiehl, and Foster 2017.
2. For more information about methods and findings, see the Montgomery College Libraries Ethnography Study (http://libguides.montgomerycollege.edu/ethnographic).
3. The pivot table feature of Excel allows the researcher to create a quick table that shows the relationship between two variables. For example, we were able to investigate whether there was any relationship between the place a student conducted academic tasks and the type of tasks the student conducted. Information about pivot tables can be found through a simple Google search, or go to the Microsoft Office support site at support.office.com and search for pivot tables.

8

Library Instruction and Academic Success

The Impact of Student Engagement
at a Community College

During fall 2013, College of Southern Nevada (CSN) librarians were working through the impact of significant changes. Earlier that year, the Nevada System of Higher Education (NSHE) had adopted a new funding formula that, for the first time, funded institutions based on student outcomes. If CSN did not meet the goals set out in this formula, up to 20 percent of its budget could be taken away in the following years (NSHE 2013). How could the librarians demonstrate our impact on student outcomes? What programs and practices would need to change? CSN Libraries also had a new director, Beth Schuck, who was dedicated to assessment, viewing it as the way to provide evidence for how the libraries are helping students be successful. As part of this focus, she challenged the librarians to come up with proposals for the ACRL Assessment in Action (AIA) program (ACRL 2017). I accepted this challenge, and put together a proposal to ascertain whether the different types of instruction that we provided have an impact on student success outcomes. Our application was approved, enabling us to participate in AIA's second-year cohort (2014/15). Our work on this project is the focus of this chapter.

INSTITUTIONAL CONTEXT

CSN is a very large commuter community college, with 34,293 students taking courses online and spread out over three campuses and seven centers throughout the Las Vegas metropolitan area (CSN Institutional Research 2016, unpublished data). It has libraries at the three campuses: Charleston (in Las Vegas), North Las Vegas, and Henderson. Although these libraries, along with their respective campuses, have their own identities and organizational cultures, they are part of one centrally administered library system, with one library director. The Charleston campus has the most students, at 14,949, compared to 10,030 at North Las Vegas, and 4,820 at Henderson (CSN Institutional Research 2016, unpublished data). These proportions are also reflected in the campus libraries' physical collections, gate counts, and circulation statistics. Most librarians and library staff work at the Charleston campus, as does CSN administration. However, each campus library provides full services to its campus community, including instruction programs.

Students at CSN are highly diverse (34 percent white, 28 percent Hispanic, 11 percent African American, 10 percent Asian, 5 percent multiracial) (NCES 2017), and many experience a variety of challenges in pursuing their academic goals. Typical of commuter college students, as described in this volume's introduction, they balance work, family, and other obligations (73 percent part-time) (NCES 2017), deal with inadequate personal finances (34 percent receive Pell grants) (NCES 2017), and may be unfamiliar with many aspects of higher education (22 percent are first-generation college students) (CSN 2016). Several of these characteristics have been associated with low completion rates (Nakajima, Dembo, and Mossler 2012), which has been consistent with the situation at CSN (7 percent three-year associate degree graduation rate; 16 percent transfer out rate) (NCES 2017).

Although there have been increasing efforts to engage students on campus as a way to improve student outcomes, these efforts are constrained by having few places for students to spend time outside of their classes. For example, only the North Las Vegas campus has an indoor recreation facility, and there are no student unions or wellness centers. This is one reason why the libraries have served as popular places for individual and group study, and as student gathering places. In fact, the three campus libraries collectively had over three quarters of a million individual visits in the 2015/16 academic year (CSN Libraries 2017). As is the case at similar commuter institutions, library spaces have a significant role in many CSN students' academic experience (Regalado and Smale 2015). At the same time, as is typical for busy commuter students who balance multiple responsibilities, the bulk of the time most students spend on campus is in classrooms (Barnett 2011). It is not unusual for librarians to hear that a student has been at CSN for several semesters and has rarely or never used library resources or set foot in a campus library. Therefore, a critical opportunity for librarians to meaningfully interact with students is through library instruction. This leads to a question that was central to CSN's AIA project: what is the impact of our instruction interactions with students on their academic success? With 10,000 students attending over 550 library instruction sessions a year (CSN Libraries 2017), CSN librarians wanted to know whether the dedication of their limited resources to this effort is leading to measurable results.

COMMUTER COMMUNITY COLLEGE LIBRARY INSTRUCTION AND STUDENT SUCCESS

In developing our AIA project, we were inspired by the Value of Academic Libraries initiative (Oakleaf 2010) and hoped to be able to correlate academic library use with student academic success, as others had done (Soria, Fransen, and Nackerud 2013; Murray, Ireland, and Hackathorn 2016). We also noted that typical one-shot instruction sessions, as provided for community college introductory-level courses, had not been shown to have a measurable impact on academic success. We wondered what factors might be important to make library instruction more effective. In seeking an answer to this question, we have been guided by Tinto's work (1997, 2000, 2012) on student engagement at commuter colleges, and others who have considered how these ideas apply to urban community college contexts (Karp, Hughes, and O'Gara 2010; Deil-Amen 2011).

Soria, Fransen, and Nackerud's (2013) research set the standard for efforts to quantify the impact of academic libraries on student success. They noted that there are positive relationships in GPA (3.18 for library users, 2.98 for non-users) and persistence for first-year students (2.9 percent who did not return in the spring for library users, 4.3 percent for non-library users) (154). In contrast, they found that course-integrated library instruction "was associated with lower grade point averages" (161). Similarly, although Murray, Ireland, and Hackathorn's (2016) study determined there to be a 9.54 odds ratio for retention for a first-semester student who uses library resources, and a 4.23 odds ratio from Spring of the first year to the following Fall semester, they found that attendance at instruction sessions had no significant relationship to student success outcomes (638).

Since significant connections have been found between the use of library services and academic success metrics, what accounts for the discrepancy between those results and the lack of measurable outcomes for instruction programs? One factor could be self-selection bias, which "may contribute to systematic differences between students who decide to use library resources and those who do not use library resources" (Soria, Fransen, and Nackerud 2017, 814). In other words, students who use library resources may already be more academically engaged than other students, which accounts for their improved outcomes. Students who attend instruction sessions, however, may do so because it is a course requirement, not due to personal motivation or interest.

Two studies that focused on library instruction at commuter community colleges, by Sanabria (2013) and Burgoyne and Chuppa-Cornell (2015), provide insight into this topic. In both studies, a library instruction component is fully integrated into a course. Sanabria describes the development and impact of the library's collaboration with Freshman-Year-Seminars (FYS) at Bronx Community College. To address low retention rates, FYS incorporate a range of high-impact practices and integrate an information literacy component. Students who participated in FYS had a retention rate from Fall to Spring of their first year of 75.2 percent compared to an overall retention rate of 50.2 percent (98). Burgoyne and Chuppa-Cornell's study of an online learning community course that combines a library research course with English 102 had similar results. Compared to the in-person version of the learning community, students had improved persistence and completion results (persistence: 85 percent compared to 77 percent; completion: 74 percent compared to 67 percent) (418). In these studies, the level of student engagement, grounded in course integration and collaboration, may be a factor in the improved student outcomes.

The question for commuter college libraries, where a full-semester course may not be an option, is whether or not what these studies indicate is effective can be scaled to a single instruction session. A starting point is to develop a better understanding of which practices have been shown to improve student outcomes. These include using active learning techniques (Braxton, Millem, and Sullivan 2000), focusing on content that is relevant and important with the "demand [that students] interact with faculty and peers about [these] substantive matters" (Kuh 2008, 14), and using collaboration with other faculty and staff to introduce "a variety of perspectives beyond that of one faculty member" (Tinto 1997, 613). Integrating these three practices—active learning, demanding content, and collaboration—into instruction sessions takes effort and forethought, requiring both a focus on pedagogy and the development of strong partnerships.

Another critical factor for student success is what happens after the instruction session. Probably every instruction librarian can recall incidents in which students she met in an instruction session subsequently consult with her regularly for research assistance or to help navigate the college bureaucracy. Deil-Amen (2011) and Karp, Hughes, and O'Gara's (2010) studies found that these connections are often critical for student success. Deil-Amen describes how such connections "provide needed support" and "enhance feelings of college belonging, college identity, and college competence" that lead to student persistence (73). Similarly, Karp, Hughes, and O'Gara examine how relationships formed through classroom interactions provide a foundation for the development of "information networks" (76). According to their findings, these "tend to be grounded in the academic discipline of the course" (81) and, once formed, prepare students to "navigate the campus environment, access knowledge about the college, create a sense of social belonging, and ultimately, [make them] feel that there are people who care about their academic welfare" (84). Brought together, these studies indicate that when an instruction session is engaging, it may both lead to improved student outcomes and serve as the springboard for connections that help a student well beyond the class meeting.

CSN'S ASSESSMENT IN ACTION PROJECT

When CSN entered into the Assessment in Action project,[1] our instruction program had, for years, been moving toward a focus on course-integrated and embedded librarian instruction. Most of the instruction librarians considered these to be best practices, since a course-integrated approach had long been supported by the Association of College & Research Libraries (2000). Not all of the instruction librarians embraced these ideas; some continued to provide library tours and general orientations. For this reason, we had two goals that we hoped to achieve in AIA. One was to show that our instruction program, overall, was making an impact on improving student success outcomes. This would be especially important for communicating the instruction program's value to the CSN administration. The second was to demonstrate that assignment-integrated library instruction is more effective than general orientations. We felt this to be critical for providing evidence and building momentum for making changes to our instruction program.

Through in-person workshops and webinars throughout the year, the AIA program helped us transform these goals into a research project. The CSN AIA team, including the head of our libraries' instructional services and technology team, Caprice Roberson, and two CSN Institutional Research analysts, one an expert on data analysis, the other on survey design, applied ideas from the AIA program and drew on their own expertise to create a quasi-experimental research design with a pretest and posttest. The project's instrument has sixteen questions on the pretest and posttest, and four additional questions only on the posttest (see appendix). The first ten questions were modified from a fifteen-question information literacy quiz that we had created in-house. Based on ACRL's *Information Literacy Competency Standards for Higher Education* (2000), these questions reflect its core concept that an information-literate person can find, evaluate, and ethically use information. The next six questions were on attitudes toward information sources, CSN's online and campus libraries, and the research process (questions 11 to 16). Three of the four questions that only appeared on the posttest were on confidence in getting better grades on course assignments, completing future assignments, and feeling connected to the college after receiving library instruction (questions 18 to

20). One posttest-only question asked students to self-report whether they had attended the library instruction session (question 17).

In order to compare the impact of our various types of instruction on student success outcomes, we included library orientations, with instructional content not directly connected to the course; assignment-integrated, with content related to completing an assignment; embedded librarian, with two or more instruction sessions and a focus on the research process; online tutorial, which assigns students to complete Research 101,[2] CSN's information literacy tutorial; and drop-in workshops, where the instructor gives the students credit for attending an introduction to research workshop. After determining which instruction types to include, we recruited six faculty who had consistently used these instruction types: four from the Department of English, one from the Department of Sociology, and one from the Department of Biological Sciences. Based on the primary campuses of the participating teaching faculty, the course sections were almost evenly split between the Charleston (seven sections) and North Las Vegas campuses (eight sections), with no sections at the Henderson campus.

During the Fall semester of 2014 we collected data. Seventeen sections participated, including one of English 100 (Composition Enhanced), two of English 101 (Composition One, a required prerequisite for many programs), six of English 102 (Composition Two), two of Biology 189 (Fundamentals of Life Science, a required 100-level biology course for many programs), and six of Sociology 101 (Principles of Sociology). All participating teaching faculty gave the pretest during the first two weeks of the semester and the posttest during the last two weeks. In the end, we had 365 students take the pretest while 221 took the posttest. I analyzed the results during the Spring semester of 2015, dividing results by the question types described above, and adding to these documented attendance at an instruction session, which we found to be more reliable than self-reported attendance. For both the attitudes on library research (questions 11 to 16) and the confidence and connectedness questions (questions 18 to 20), we created index variables to discover if there were any significant relationships between results for these question types and student success outcomes.

RESULTS AND INTERPRETATION

The results of CSN's AIA project confirmed previous research from Tinto, Kuh, and others that more engaging instruction is related to improved student outcomes. Specifically, the results for individual instruction types fall along a continuum, with instruction with less student engagement having weaker results and more engaging instruction having stronger results. Another finding is that there is an overall link between student participation in CSN's library instruction program and academic success (table 8.1).

TABLE 8.1

Significant correlations and results

	INSTRUCTION TYPE					
	Library orientation	Online tutorial	Drop-in workshop	Assignment integrated	Embedded librarian	Overall
Confidence index variable with course grade correlation	-.25	NA	.27*	.34*	.66*	.28*
Sig. (2-tailed)	.17		.03	.04	.04	.00
n (posttest)	32		70	37	10	155
Confidence index variable with term GPA correlation	-.11	.12	.29*	.55*	.54	.23*
Sig. (2-tailed)	.56	.59	.02	.00	.11	.00
n (posttest)	32	22	71	37	10	178
Attendance with term GPA correlation	.08	NA	.23*	.39*	NA	.30*
Sig. (2-tailed)	.57		.02	.00		.00
n (pretest)	48		108	61		217
Correct increase (%) between pretest and posttest for MLA citation identification	-16.0	24.0	-12.0	-1.0	61.0	-4.0
n (pretest, posttest)	47, 35	38, 23	142, 98	68, 40	45, 10	362, 219
Correct increase (%) between pretest and posttest for information literacy questions	4.4	4.5	3.2	-1.0	21.1	3.5
n (posttest)	34	22	88	40	9	193
Number of correct posttest information literacy questions with term GPA correlation	-.35*	.43*	.33*	-.17	.11	.09
Sig. (2-tailed)	.05	.04	.00	.29	.77	.21
n (posttest)	34	22	75	39	10	186

*Correlations are significant at the .05 level.

NA: The result cannot be computed because at least one of the variables is constant.

Attendance at an Instruction Session

The most important overall finding was a weak, but significant correlation between attendance at an instruction session and semester grades. This indicates that something positive for student success may be happening in the instruction sessions; however, it could also be that students who come to class do better than students who do not. The results for the specific instruction types, however, lead to a more nuanced conclusion. There was no significant correlation between attending a general library orientation and semester grades, for example, while there were weak, but significant correlations between attending a drop-in workshop or an assignment-integrated instruction session and semester grades. These results indicate that instruction types may be associated with disparate student outcomes.

Confidence and Connectedness

The correlations between the confidence and connectedness index variable, and course and semester grades reinforce the association of student outcomes with instruction type. This variable, representing students' self-reported confidence in doing their academic work and feeling of connection to CSN after an instruction session, tells us about the perceived impact of library instruction. Though students certainly can be overconfident about their academic skills and their ability to do academic research (Gross and Latham 2012), linking this variable to student success outcomes grounds these results in academic performance.

Overall, there were weak, positive correlations between the confidence and connectedness index variable and both the course grade and term GPA. Similar to instruction session attendance, there were no significant correlations between this index variable and the library orientation or information literacy tutorial cohorts. Close to the overall results, the drop-in workshop group also had weak, significant correlations to both course grades and semester GPA. Stronger correlations with this variable were seen in the assignment-integrated and embedded librarian cohorts. For the former, the correlation with course grade was higher, but still in the weak range, while for semester GPA, it was in the moderate range. For the embedded librarian cohort, there was a strong correlation to course grade.

Information Literacy and Attitudes on Library Research

Unlike the picture that emerged from the data on attendance and confidence and connectedness, the results from the information literacy and attitudes on library research questions were more opaque. While there were no overall significant correlations to academic success outcomes for either question category, the results tell us something about what students learned from the instruction

TABLE 8.2

Chi squared (χ^2) significant change: information literacy and attitudes questions

	INSTRUCTION TYPE					
	Library orientation	Online tutorial	Drop-in workshop	Assignment integrated	Embedded librarian	Overall
QUESTION 1: χ^2	5.77	1.70	2.72	7.25	10.74*	3.43
Sig. (2-tailed)	.12	.64	.44	.06	.01	.33
n	83	61	239	110	56	584
QUESTION 5: χ^2	2.37	5.50	11.65*	4.16	9.82*	26.57*
Sig. (2-tailed)	.30	.06	.01	.09	.01	.00
n	83	61	241	109	56	585
QUESTION 6: χ^2	3.72	3.33	.770	1.16	5.66	5.60*
Sig. (2-tailed)	.156	.19	.681	.56	.06	.05
n	83	61	241	108	56	582
QUESTION 7: χ^2	6.64	3.73	5.99	3.15	12.78*	3.91
Sig. (2-tailed)	.08	.15	.11	.37	.01	.42
n	82	61	240	108	55	581
QUESTION 12: χ^2	1.18	7.03	17.71*	9.47*	8.25*	31.92*
Sig. (2-tailed)	.76	.07	.00	.02	.04	.00
n	83	61	241	109	56	583
Question 13: χ^2	.395	1.15	8.45*	10.14*	.61	14.65*
Sig. (2-tailed)	.94	.56	.04	.02	.90	.00
n	67	51	188	86	28	448
Question 15: χ^2	3.57	6.15	10.33*	.85	.344	5.63
Sig. (2-tailed)	.311	.11	.02	.66	.84	.13
n	63	51	171	87	28	431
Question 16: χ^2	4.96	5.99*a	4.37	3.24	4.73	11.60*
Sig. (2-tailed)	.18	.01	.22	.36	.19	.01
n	71	52	186	91	29	457

NOTE: Question text is in the appendix.

*Chi squared values are significant at the .05 level.

[a]Fisher's exact test used to verify significance.

sessions, and what attitudes toward library research changed. They also provide more context to the overall finding on the impact of instruction type. For both question types, we used Pearson's chi-squared tests to identify whether there were significant changes from the pretest to posttest. The results for questions with significant positive change in at least one instruction type or overall are included in table 8.2.

Information Literacy

For the information literacy questions, there were overall positive, significant changes from pretest to posttest in two out of ten questions: number 5, on how to find an academic journal article and 6 on choosing a topic. Although it is encouraging to see these improvements, the lack of measurable impacts on the other eight questions is somewhat alarming. Generally, since librarians focus on whichever information literacy concepts they consider relevant in a particular course section, it would be unrealistic to expect that more than a few would be covered in a given session. These results reflect both librarians' content discretion and a lack of alignment between instructional content and the AIA instrument's questions.

In looking at the individual instruction types, the results paralleled the patterns seen in the confidence and connectedness questions, with some differences. Starting with the weakest results, the library orientation group had no significant positive results for information literacy questions, though on average students improved by 4.4 percent between pretest and posttest in this cohort, comparable to or slightly stronger than most other groups. Doing somewhat better, the online tutorial group scored above average on most information literacy questions, but on question seven, which asked students to identify an MLA book citation, the results for this cohort were 28 percent better than average. For most of the other sections, with the exception of the embedded librarian group, the scores declined for this question, indicating that we do citation instruction better in an online tutorial than in a one-shot session.

Another significant result for this group was a moderate correlation between the posttest score on information literacy questions and term GPA. A parallel result is seen in the drop-in workshop cohort, which had a slightly weaker correlation. This relationship, being only from the posttest score, doesn't tell us that the student learned anything from the instruction session. It seems to indicate, instead, that for students who made an effort to attend a workshop or complete a tutorial, the information literacy concepts they retained had some connection to their overall academic performance.

Unlike the solid correlations with confidence and connectedness seen in the assignment-integrated cohort, for information literacy skills questions, assignment-integrated instruction performed the worst of all instruction types. With a 1 percent decline in scores from pretest to posttest and no significant improvements, this cohort contrasted with the embedded librarian program, which did well in both information literacy and confidence. The latter group averaged a 21.1 percent improvement in information literacy scores and saw significant improvement in question 1, on types of search; and questions 5 and 7, summarized above. These results indicate that the content learned by the assignment-integrated cohort, while helpful in boosting confidence, was unrelated to this metric. The embedded librarian program could do well in both question categories because of planning—forethought was given to how course assignments reinforce information literacy skills—and additional practice time, making it more likely for concepts to move from short-term to long-term memory.

Attitudes on Library Research

For the attitudes on library research questions, significant results reflect broad themes in the instruction program and the unique characteristics of particular cohorts. Of the six questions, three had significant positive change overall and in one or more instruction type. Question 12, whether students know how to find and use appropriate sources for assignments, had the most widespread positive change, overall and in three cohorts: drop-in workshop, assignment-integrated, and embedded librarian. Since one of the instruction program's main goals has been to help students complete assignments, these improvements indicate that students perceived there to be an impact in this area. For question 13, knowing how to find resources needed for assignments on the CSN library website, significant change was seen overall, and in the drop-in workshop and assignment-integrated cohorts. This result makes sense in that using online library resources to complete assignments is a consistent focus of the instruction program. For question 16, whether students view the library website as user-friendly, significant positive change was seen overall and in the online tutorial cohort. This may reflect the fact that the cohort's primary interaction with the library was online.

Unique results were seen in the drop-in workshop and embedded librarian cohorts. The former is the only cohort to have a significant result for question 15, on whether or not the library staff is approachable. Perhaps going to a workshop as opposed to a librarian coming to their class led to a positive view of librarian accessibility. The embedded librarian group was unique in that the change from pretest to posttest for the attitudes questions strongly correlated with course grade. This represents a connection between these questions and student success outcomes. Like the information literacy questions, this may reflect that it takes time, which is often absent in one-shot sessions, for students to internalize changes in attitudes.

Student Engagement and Instruction Type

Overall, increased course integration and student engagement were linked to improved confidence, institutional connectedness, and grades. For the library orientation group, the lack of significant positive results seemed to be based on minimal student engagement. Merely talking about library resources without connecting the content in a meaningful way to a student's academic work did not lead to more confidence or connection to the college, content retention, or attitudinal change. For the online tutorial instruction type, the absence of significant correlations with confidence and institutional connectedness may reflect the lack of one-on-one interactions with librarians, which may reinforce academic research skills and thereby boost confidence.

Making sense of the results for the assignment-integrated one-shot library instruction is critical because this instruction type represents a more engaging alternative to a traditional library orientation, while being less resource-intensive than an embedded librarian program. We would argue that this type of instruction involves the three characteristics of student engagement in a one-shot instruction session described above: active learning, to engage students in creative ways to complete an assignment; demanding content, when the instruction session is grounded in a challenging assignment; and collaboration, which is at the heart of an effective assignment-integrated instruction session. The positive results connected to confidence and connectedness paired with weak results for information literacy point not necessarily to a failing of this approach, but to the need for an alternative to using generic information literacy questions for assessing its effectiveness.

Lastly, the embedded librarian cohort did better than any other in most measures. These results reflect the high level of student engagement and course integration in this instruction type. Specifically, the librarian met with students multiple times over the course of the semester and led them through the research process in connection to completing an assignment. The intensity of the librarian's involvement in the course, however, has led to challenges scaling up this type of instruction, both due to difficulty recruiting faculty and to the time commitment required of librarians.

LIMITATIONS

One of the goals of the Assessment in Action program is to build librarians' research skills. CSN librarians did not necessarily begin their projects as expert researchers; instead, we learned as we worked on our projects. Among other challenges, this is connected to a significant limitation of this study: the pretest and posttest instruments were not validated or tested on students before use to check for confusing wording or jargon. Another limitation is that some participating sections had small sample sizes that limited the usefulness of the data and caused us to remove the online course with drop-in workshop data from the instruction type results. Finally, CSN students, though similar in some ways to their peers at other urban commuter community colleges, are also unique demographically and socioeconomically. Although we hope that this work inspires others to build on our research, for this reason our findings may not be generalizable beyond their applications at CSN.

CHANGES TO THE INSTRUCTION PROGRAM

CSN's AIA project was officially completed with a poster session at the 2015 ALA Annual Conference,[3] but the process of understanding the implications of our findings had just begun. During the summer of 2015, the project's results and recommendations were presented to all CSN librarians. From their responses, it became clear that to make changes based on AIA results we needed to confront issues related to campus cultures, working relationships with faculty, and long-standing workflows. While many of us were already committed to assignment-integrated instruction and to building an embedded librarian program, others were reluctant to embrace this direction.

While continuing to work toward full buy-in, we decided to act. One change was to relabel non-assignment-focused library orientations as marketing events, excluding them from instruction data. Another was to require that all instruction be course-related with identified student learning outcomes (SLOs). This change enabled us to make SLOs the focus of instruction assessment. Emerging from the AIA finding that general information literacy skills often do not align with assignment-integrated instruction session content, we have found that focusing on SLOs is more responsive to the particular course and assignment. Another change inspired by our findings is that the SLO assessment instrument we developed includes both information literacy and confidence-related questions.

The impressive results from the embedded librarian program challenged us to find more faculty willing to work with librarians in this way. Recruiting has been successful; we have seen a large influx from a new online embedded librarian program, now with over twenty sections. This program leverages the strengths of online tutorials, as seen in the AIA results on specific information literacy and attitudes questions, with the student engagement of an embedded librarian program. Finally, although the AIA results support our continuing drop-in workshops, this was based on how the AIA participating course using this instruction type reinforced library workshop content. In general, however, workshop attendance has been mainly from students seeking extra credit from courses that did not provide this reinforcement. Therefore, we have stopped offering workshops, except when they have a particular theme, such as citations.

CONCLUSIONS AND FUTURE DIRECTIONS

When we consider the ways that academic libraries at commuter colleges impact student success outcomes, the results of this study indicate that our focus should be on how we can most effectively engage students, especially those who are not predisposed to be library users. Significant relationships can be found between the use of library services and academic success metrics, as many studies have indicated. However, it would be disingenuous if we did not consider the role of self-selection bias among students who choose to use these resources. A greater challenge than finding correlations between library use and student outcomes is to change the trajectory of students who may not have otherwise taken advantage of library resources at all.

Many commuter college students may be too busy and preoccupied with other concerns to spend much time considering what library resources may be available to them and how those resources may help them with their academic work. Students can make it through academic programs with limited exposure to library resources. Instruction programs are one way that librarians can meaningfully interact with such students. If a student makes a connection to a librarian or to the content of the library instruction session, and especially if that content is personally and academically relevant to them, they may experience a "socio-academic integrative moment" (Deil-Amen 2011). In addition to classrooms, these moments could occur at the reference desk, at events outside the library, or online. After such moments, students may go on to become library users and to include librarians in their information networks (Karp, Hughes, and O'Gara 2010). Quite possibly, what begins in the classroom can translate into increased confidence and institutional connectedness, may influence decisions to persist with academic work, and may make a difference in students' overall academic and life paths.

It is important to also note that such moments are not necessarily going to occur simply because the instruction session is engaging. What may matter just as much is that the instructional content "be grounded in the academic discipline of the course" (Karp, Hughes, and O'Gara 2010, 81). Course integration seems to be the key. Connecting with students through their academic work makes it possible for personal connections to develop, and increases the likelihood of a commuter student connecting to the college in a meaningful and impactful way.

At CSN, further exploring which factors in library instruction and student engagement make an impact on student success has been ongoing work. For two years we have applied insights from AIA to develop a three-question instrument, used in our most common library instruction courses, to assess if students improved their information literacy skills and confidence based on one-shot instruction sessions. Outside of the instruction program and beyond the library's walls, we have expanded our efforts at student engagement by connecting to students around issues important to them. Recently, we have cosponsored and participated in events related to Black Lives Matter and undocumented students, and coordinated a Human Library event focused on student diversity. A question for further research is how these ways of engaging students at commuter colleges connect to improving student success outcomes.

Another area for further research will be to test ideas expressed by Karp, Hughes, and O'Gara (2010) and Deil-Amen (2011). What does it mean to students for a librarian to be part of their information network? How can we facilitate students having socio-academic integrative moments? We speculate that the lack of a residential component increases the importance of librarians serving in these roles at commuter institutions. We plan to explore this topic through qualitative research in the coming years.

Viewing our role from a student engagement perspective is just one lens to understand broader questions of how we can improve student outcomes. What seems to be critical to why confidence and connectedness emerged as themes in the CSN AIA project is that they address affective barriers to using library resources. Such barriers include library anxiety, which may be more prevalent among students likely to attend commuter institutions (Lee 2012), and low levels of academic research self-efficacy, which are often related to a lack of similar previous experience. Further research should focus on how and what types of student engagement at academic libraries serving commuter students can reduce these and other non-cognitive barriers to student success.

REFERENCES

ACRL (Association of College & Research Libraries). 2000. *Information Literacy Competency Standards for Higher Education*. Chicago: American Library Association. www.ala.org/acrl/sites/ala.org.acrl/files/content/standards/standards.pdf.

———. 2017. "Assessment in Action: Academic Libraries and Student Success." www.ala.org/acrl/AIA.

Barnett, Elisabeth A. 2011. "Validation Experiences and Persistence among Community College Students." *The Review of Higher Education* 34 (2): 193–230. doi:10.1353/rhe.2010.0019.

Braxton, John M., Jeffrey F. Milem, and Anna Shaw Sullivan. 2000. "The Influence of Active Learning on the College Student Departure Process: Toward a Revision of Tinto's Theory." *The Journal of Higher Education* 71 (5): 569–90. doi:10.1080/00221546.2000.11778853.

Burgoyne, Mary Beth, and Kim Chuppa-Cornell. 2015. "Beyond Embedded: Creating an Online-Learning Community Integrating Information Literacy and Composition Courses." *The Journal of Academic Librarianship* 41 (4): 416–21. doi:10.1016/j.acalib.2015.05.005.

Chodock, Ted. 2017. "College of Southern Nevada: Project Description." ACRL: Assessment in Action. https://apply.ala.org/aia/docs/project/10171.

CSN. 2016. "College of Southern Nevada." Last modified December 7. https://www
.csn.edu/sites/default/files/csn_metro_highered_preso.pdf.

CSN Libraries. 2017. "About CSN Library Services." http://sites.csn.edu/library/
about/dashboard.html.

Deil-Amen, Regina. 2011. "Socio-Academic Integrative Moments: Rethinking
Academic and Social Integration among Two-Year College Students in Career-
Related Programs." *The Journal of Higher Education* 82 (1): 54–91. doi:10.1080/0
0221546.2011.11779085.

Gross, Melissa, and Don Latham. 2012. "What's Skills Got to Do with It? Information
Literacy Skills and Self-Views of Ability among First-Year College Students."
Journal of the American Society for Information Science and Technology 63 (3):
574–83. doi:10.1002/asi.21681.

Karp, Melinda Mechur, Katherine L. Hughes, and Lauren O'Gara. 2010. "An
Exploration of Tinto's Integration Framework for Community College Students."
The Journal of College Student Retention 12 (1): 69–86. doi:10.2190/CS.12.1.e.

Kuh, George D. 2008. *High-Impact Educational Practices: What They Are, Who Has
Access to Them, and Why They Matter*. Washington, DC: Association of American
Colleges and Universities.

Lee, Scott W. 2012. "An Exploratory Study of Library Anxiety in Developmental
Education Students." *Community and Junior College Libraries* 18 (2): 67–87. doi:1
0.1080/02763915.2012.726806.

Murray, Adam, Ashley Ireland, and Jana Hackathorn. 2016. "The Value of Academic
Libraries: Library Services as a Predictor of Student Retention." *College and
Research Libraries* 77 (5): 631–42. doi:10.5860/crl.77.5.631.

Nakajima, Mikiko A., Myron H. Dembo, and Ron Mossler. 2012. "Student Persistence
in Community Colleges." *Community College Journal of Research and Practice* 36
(8): 591–613. doi:10.1080/10668920903054931.

National Center for Education Statistics (NCES). 2017. "College Navigator: College
of Southern Nevada." IES>NCES National Center for Education Statistics.
https://nces.ed.gov/collegenavigator/?s=NV&zc=89146&zd=0&of=3&1=92&ts
=NV&id=182005.

NSHE (Nevada System of Higher Education). 2013. *A New Funding Formula for
Higher Education*. Las Vegas, NV: Nevada System of Higher Education, http://
system.nevada.edu/tasks/sites/Nshe/assets/File/Initiatives/fundingformula/
Formula%20Funding%20Update%20-%2004–10–13.pdf.

Oakleaf, Megan. 2010. *The Value of Academic Libraries: A Comprehensive Research
Review and Report*. Chicago: American Library Association.

Regalado, Mariana, and Maura A. Smale. 2015. "'I Am More Productive in the Library
Because It's Quiet': Commuter Students in the College Library." *College and
Research Libraries* 76 (7): 899–913. doi:10.5860/crl.76.7.899.

Sanabria, Jesus E. 2013. "The Library as an Academic Partner in Student Retention
and Graduation: The Library's Collaboration with the Freshman Year Seminar

Initiative at the Bronx Community College." *Collaborative Librarianship* 5 (2): 94–100. http://digitalcommons.du.edu/collaborativelibrarianship/vol5/iss2/4/.

Soria, Krista M., Jan Fransen, and Shane Nackerud. 2013. "Library Use and Undergraduate Outcomes: New Evidence for Students' Retention and Academic Success." *portal: Libraries and the Academy* 13 (2): 147–64. doi:10.1353/pla.2013.0010.

———. 2017. "The Impact of Academic Library Resources on Undergraduates' Degree Completion." *College and Research Libraries* 78 (6): 812–23. doi:10.5860/crl.78.6.812.

Tinto, Vincent. 1997. "Classrooms as Communities: Exploring the Educational Character of Student Persistence." *The Journal of Higher Education* 68 (6): 599–623. doi:10.1080/00221546.1997.11779003.

———. 2000. "Linking Learning and Leaving: Exploring the Role of the College Classroom in Student Departure." In *Reworking the Student Departure Puzzle*, edited by John M. Braxton, 81–94. Nashville, TN: Vanderbilt University Press.

———. 2012. "Enhancing Student Success: Taking the Classroom Success Seriously." *The International Journal of the First Year in Higher Education* 3 (1): 1–8. doi:10.5204/intjfyhe.v2i1.119.

U.S. Department of Education. 2017. "Library Statistics Program: Compare Academic Libraries: 2012-College of Southern Nevada." IES>NCES: National Center for Education Statistics. https://nces.ed.gov/surveys/libraries/compare/LCFinalReport_New.aspx?RptID=Adhoc.

APPENDIX

CSN's Assessment in Action Instrument: Posttest Version

QUESTION TYPES

- One to ten: information literacy skills; on pretest and posttest
- Eleven to sixteen: attitudes toward information sources, CSN's online and campus libraries, and the research process; on pretest and posttest; responses combined for index variable
- Seventeen: attendance at an instruction session; on posttest only
- Eighteen to twenty: confidence in getting better grades on course assignments, completing future assignments, and feeling connected to the college after receiving library instruction; on posttest only; responses combined for index variable

CSN Library Services—Assessment in Action #2

For the following questions,
please circle the letter to indicate the correct answer.

1. The broadest type of search, which looks for your terms anywhere, is:

    A. Subject search

    B. Title search

    C. Author search

    D. Keyword search

2. You are looking for American high school dropout statistics to support an argument in a research paper you are writing. Which source would be best for locating the most current statistic?

    A. A book about education in America

    B. The U.S. Department of Education website

    C. A journal article about a teacher performance evaluation

    D. An encyclopedia article about a high school dropout

3. Which of the following is NOT a consideration in evaluating the credibility of information found in a source?

    A. Relevance—answers your question

    B. Currency—up-to-date information

    C. Authority—expertise of the author

    D. Objectivity—unbiased information

4. Paraphrasing, or summarizing the words and ideas of someone else, without giving credit in your research paper is considered plagiarism:

   A. True

   B. False

5. You need to find current journal articles about stem cell research for a biology class. What is the best way to get started?

   A. Browse the library shelves

   B. Search for websites using Google

   C. Use a library research database

   D. Search the library catalog for books on stem cell research

6. You are writing a 4–5 page research paper and are thinking of writing about the following topic: *What are the causes of obesity?* This topic is:

   A. Too narrow

   B. Too broad

   C. Neither

7. The following MLA citation is an example of what type of information source?

   Bryson, Robert. *Evolution: A Historical Perspective.* New York: Greenwood Press, 2008. Print.

   A. Magazine article

   B. Book

   C. Website

   D. Newspaper article

8. You are writing a paper on climate change, but you first need to find a brief definition of "greenhouse gases" for your introduction. What would be the best source for finding some credible, brief background information?

   A. Search for journal articles about "greenhouse gases"

   B. Search for books on climate change in the library catalog

   C. Look up "greenhouse gases" in an online encyclopedia or dictionary through the CSN Library Services website

   D. Use a search engine to locate websites that mention "greenhouse gases"

9. Class debate topic: "Should online poker be legalized?" What are the two most important keywords or phrases you would use to search for information on this topic?

    A. Poker and Internet

    B. Compulsive gambling and online poker

    C. Online poker and legalize

    D. Tax revenue and gambling

10. Information you find on the Internet:

    A. Comes from a variety of sources, such as business, the government, or private citizens

    B. Is much more reliable than books, magazines, and journals

    C. Is required by international law to be accurate, current, and unbiased

    D. Is factual since Internet content is monitored by the World Wide Web Consortium (W3C)

For the following questions,
please check [x] the box to indicate your response.

11. I am critical of the quality of web sites and other sources that I use for assignments.

    [ ] strongly disagree

    [ ] somewhat disagree

    [ ] somewhat agree

    [ ] strongly agree

12. I know how to find and use appropriate sources for my assignments.

    [ ] strongly disagree

    [ ] somewhat disagree

    [ ] somewhat agree

    [ ] strongly agree

13. Finding resources I need for assignments on the CSN library website is

    [ ] very difficult

    [ ] somewhat difficult

    [ ] somewhat easy

    [ ] very easy

    [ ] never used it for that purpose

14. Finding resources I need in one of the CSN campus libraries (Charleston, Cheyenne, or Henderson) is

    [ ] very difficult

    [ ] somewhat difficult

    [ ] somewhat easy

    [ ] very easy

    [ ] never used it for that purpose

15. The library staff are approachable

    [ ] strongly disagree

    [ ] somewhat disagree

    [ ] somewhat agree

    [ ] strongly agree

    [ ] don't know/never interacted with them

16. The library website is user-friendly

    [ ] strongly disagree

    [ ] somewhat disagree

    [ ] somewhat agree

    [ ] strongly agree

    [ ] don't know/never used it

17. As part of this course, I received library instruction (in class, at a workshop, or online).

    [ ] Yes

    [ ] No

18. The library instruction I received (in class, at a workshop, or online) has helped me improve my grades on assignments in this course.

    [ ] strongly disagree

    [ ] somewhat disagree

    [ ] somewhat agree

    [ ] strongly agree

    [ ] don't know/did not receive instruction

19. In the future, the library instruction I received in this course (in class, at a workshop, or online) will help me complete assignments.

[ ] strongly disagree

[ ] somewhat disagree

[ ] somewhat agree

[ ] strongly agree

[ ] don't know/did not receive instruction

20. Based on my contact with a librarian, I feel more connected to CSN.

[ ] strongly disagree

[ ] somewhat disagree

[ ] somewhat agree

[ ] strongly agree

[ ] don't know/never had contact with a librarian

NOTES

1. This project was part of the program "Assessment in Action: Academic Libraries and Student Success," undertaken by the Association of College & Research Libraries in partnership with the Association for Institutional Research and the Association of Public and Land-Grant Universities. The program, a cornerstone of ACRL's Value of Academic Libraries initiative, was made possible by the Institute of Museum and Library Services.
2. CSN's Research 101 tutorial can be found here: http://libguides.csn.edu/research-101/.
3. A link to the CSN AIA poster is on the CSN Libraries website and can be accessed here: https://sites.csn.edu/library/docs/CSN_Assessment_in_Action_Poster_June_2015.pdf.

MARIANA REGALADO and
MAURA A. SMALE

9
Lessons Learned from Our Commuter Students

L ike the students who participated in the studies described in this volume, a majority of undergraduates commute to attend college in the United States, and the realities and constraints of commuting can be a significant component of their days. Commuter student demographics underscore the real-life complexities faced by many undergraduates who commute. They are likely to share at least one of these characteristics: be in the first generation of their families to attend college; be members of low-income households or are students of color; be immigrants, parents, or caregivers; or work full-time outside of college. As the institutions included in this volume exemplify, they also likely attend publicly funded colleges and universities. Learning about this "overlooked majority" can help us better serve commuter students in our libraries, and encourage their persistence and success in college. Supporting the success of our commuter students is integral to the mission of academic libraries and our commitment to social justice, as we work to enable students to participate fully as students, workers, members of their communities, and citizens of an increasingly complex world.

This volume has brought together studies with commuter students from librarians and researchers in academic libraries from around the United States, filling a gap in the higher education and library literature that has focused largely on traditional, residential students. Across our different institutions—urban and suburban, with varying enrollments and degrees offered, from solely commuter to a mix of commuter and residential students—these studies reveal important insights about the commuter student experience, and where the library fits in (or does not). Common to the student experience is the centrality of the commute, and students' need to carry their belongings throughout the day. For librarians and researchers, collaboration and advocacy both inside the library and outside the library, across the institution, surfaced as a unifying theme underlying successful support for students.

The commute is central to students' academic, and nonacademic, lives, and Clark's (2006, 3) insight that "the act of commuting in itself is a prominent feature of commuter students' college experience" cannot be overstated. While the mode of transportation can vary widely between students at different institutions, the commute—and the time and place it occupies in students' days—is responsible in large part for shaping their days in college. Commuter students spend much time strategizing their transportation to and from campus. Some students may use some of the time they spend on the commute to do their schoolwork, as many CUNY students did on public transportation. While some California community college students even found ways to study in their cars, most who drive may find they cannot use their commuting time for schoolwork as well. For other students, the expenses of commuting can be a burden, especially for those who must drive to and park on (or near) campus, a reality we heard about from students at institutions as varied as IUPUI, UNC Charlotte, and Modesto Junior College. Free shuttle bus service is surely appreciated at those campuses where it exists, such as at CU Boulder. Furthermore, the need to pay for transportation to campus can require students to take on additional employment that similarly takes time away from their studies, as we heard from a student at UNC Charlotte.

Without a dormitory to return to during the course of a typical day of classes and other commitments, commuter undergraduates have a different relationship to the physical place of their college or university than do residential students, no matter what the campus layout is. The importance of place to the commuter students at each of the institutions in this volume is strongly apparent in these studies, even for students at an online school like Coastline Community College. Students who commute must carry their belongings with them all day, and they appreciate services on campus and in the library that can literally lighten their loads, for example, course textbooks on reserve, laptop loans, and lockers. All students need access to a range of spaces for homework and studying, but commuter students may especially value campus spaces since their home or other off-campus locations may not be conducive to academic work. Again, time emerges as a critical factor that intersects with space: commuter students often fit their studying into the time between classes or other on-campus activities, and it is important that they be able to find a suitable study space in the time they have available.

Librarians and library researchers are collaborative by nature, and it is not surprising that all of the studies included in this book highlight the benefits of collaborating inside and outside of the library in doing this work. The authors are all interested first and foremost in using what they learned about students "to develop meaningful programs and services to meet their needs," as Tanner Wray of Montgomery College told us. At CU Boulder and CUNY the results from studies have been used to adjust and strengthen existing services and provide support for new projects going forward. Ted Chodock highlighted the anticipation he felt in approaching his research with CSN students: "a combination of fear that what we had been doing in our instruction program had no impact on students, and hope that we would find that specific forms of instruction led to students being more successful." Indeed, at CSN the results of the study have been used to initiate conversations in the library about how instruction can be modified to best serve their students.

A number of the researchers found themselves with opportunities to collaborate outside of their library. The Modesto and Coastline authors worked closely with their local institutional research offices, and Ted Chodock also noted to us how crucial CSN institutional research assistance was in undertaking their AIA project. Tanner Wray experienced many benefits of involving stakeholders across three community college campuses in their research. He mentioned that an "advantage to such a large-scale effort is that individuals outside the libraries develop a deeper understanding of the role of libraries in supporting student success, and a deeper understanding of our students." At IUPUI, their research has illuminated the differences between what campus planners may envision for a library and what students actually need. Sara Lowe noted that the vision of administrators "was wildly different from what students want. So the primary value of this work to the campus is that it gave us data so we do not betray students' needs."

Beyond the research process itself, identifying offices and departments across campus with which to partner can bolster advocacy for efforts to improve the commuter student experience in the library. The example of the Family Friendly Library Room at UNC Charlotte is a model for a project that grew organically out of collaboration between two campus units. The librarians from Modesto and Coastline have approached the broader California community college library community to share their results and collaborate on further research across their vast system. Building partnerships outside the library can contribute to improvements in academic and student support on campus, and can encourage commuter student success. Additionally, advocacy may provide a basis for justifying changes to the physical plant, renovation, expansion, or other costly capital projects.

Perhaps most importantly, the research in this volume demonstrates the value of listening to students' experiences and ideas. Our commuter students, like all undergraduates, have busy lives. We see them when they visit our libraries, when they are studying and doing homework, and using technology and library resources. We see them on campus, too, sitting in hallways or lounging outside or in other spots. However, we know that commuter students spend less time on campus than do residential students. What are our commuter undergraduates doing when not on campus? How do they interact with the library? How can we help them make the most of the time they do spend on campus, and provide services for when they are off campus, as well? Research on our students' experiences is key to exploring the answers to these questions. The data we gather suggests creative solutions and ensures that the best possible decisions are made, resisting trends in libraries and higher education that ultimately may not suit our students.

WHAT COMES NEXT?
Suggestions for Future Research

The research projects included in this volume have illuminated much about the successes and challenges of commuter students at eight varied institutions in the United States, and point to ways in which academic libraries can better serve them. The results of these projects—especially the similarities and differences between results at these eight institutions—can also inspire avenues for future research with commuter students at other institutions.

We have seen in many of these studies that the commute sometimes occupies significant time in students' days. More research into the commute itself could reveal modes of commuting that may vary between institutions, and how commuting impacts how students do their work. Is the financial impact of commuting a barrier for students, and can the institution take steps to mitigate that? Are there changes that colleges and universities can make that will enable students to reclaim their commute time to use for academic work? It may also be useful to consider online learning initiatives—which are on the rise at many institutions—through a commuter lens. At Coastline, students did report studying on campus though most are enrolled in online courses, and at CUNY we have heard from students that they do most of their work for blended or online courses at computer labs on campus. Are there changes in the implementation of online learning at our institutions that could make it easier for students to avoid a commute to campus?

Involving students in the gathering and analyzing of data, as they did at Montgomery College, allows for collaboration with faculty and classes across campus. Tanner Wray highlighted important benefits of the library's work with students in anthropology and architecture courses: "Watching these students hone their professional skills and seeing them do presentations on their work was extremely moving. Administrators reflected frequently on the impact on our students—not just the library users, but also these professionals in training." Commuter students often spend less time on campus than their residential counterparts, and including students as researchers can also create "additional ways for the library to become a lab for our students." While the project at Montgomery College was very large, even small-scale projects can increase opportunities for students to participate in campus life in new and useful ways.

Given the current funding climate in both libraries and higher education more broadly, especially at public colleges and universities, further research on commuter students might focus more intentionally on the ways in which academic librarians and libraries contribute to student success. This may be of particular interest in community colleges, since as Ted Chodock suggests, "without being able to justify expenses based on supporting faculty research, community college libraries increasingly have to demonstrate that they are helping students be successful." The Association of College & Research Libraries' Value of Academic Libraries and Assessment in Action projects have compiled much research on assessing the contribution of libraries to the academic success mission of the institution, but there has been little work specifically on commuter students. Tanner Wray notes that "demonstrating clearly how our programs and services contribute to efforts to dramatically improve student success is the key research and assessment need for the libraries at my institution."

Understanding our own students on our own campus is important for developing local improvements and initiatives. At the same time, while local contexts differ, there are similarities in the experiences of commuter students even across institutions in various locations and with different institutional characteristics and student demographics. Thus it is also important that we pay "more and mindful attention to the long-term work being done by other institutions" (Lanclos and Asher 2016). Comparative, collaborative research into the experiences of commuter students in academic libraries across colleges and universities can further illuminate the lived experiences of commuter students in our libraries and institutions.

We invite you to consider the place of the library and college in the lives of commuter students, to understand how being students intertwines with the larger complexities of their lives. The more we can learn about our commuter students, the more our academic libraries can consider initiatives to bolster their success on our campuses and beyond.

REFERENCES

Clark, Marcia Roe. 2006. "Succeeding in the City: Challenges and Best Practices on Urban Commuter Campuses." *About Campus* 11 (3): 2–8. doi:10.1002/abc.166.

Lanclos, Donna M., and Andrew D. Asher. 2016. "'Ethnographish:' The State of the Ethnography in Libraries." *Weave: Journal of Library User Experience* 1 (5). doi:10.3998/weave.12535642.0001.503.

Contributors

MARIANA REGALADO is an associate professor at Brooklyn College, City University of New York, where, as head of reference, she assists students to become curious and confident information seekers. Her academic background in both anthropology and library science is brought together in her research on how undergraduates perceive and conduct the research process. She has published and presented locally and nationally on her research. With Maura Smale, she is the coauthor of *Digital Technology as Affordance and Barrier in Higher Education* (2017).

MAURA A. SMALE is a professor and chief librarian at the New York City College of Technology, City University of New York, where she works with library faculty and staff to support and encourage the City Tech community in their academic pursuits. Her background includes degrees in anthropology and library and information science. With Mariana Regalado, she is the coauthor of *Digital Technology as Affordance and Barrier in Higher Education* (2017). She has researched and published on student scholarly habits, critical librarianship, game-based learning, and open education.

JEAN AMARAL is an assistant professor and open knowledge librarian at Borough of Manhattan Community College, City University of New York, where she partners with faculty across disciplines to create active and engaging learning experiences for students through open knowledge practices, such as open educational resources and Wikipedia edit-a-thons. Her research focuses on student and faculty information needs and seeking, open knowledge practices, future libraries, student technology use, and servant leadership.

TED CHODOCK is a reference and instructional services librarian at the College of Southern Nevada, where he served as lead librarian for CSN's Assessment in Action project. Previously he was a research services librarian at Landmark College in Vermont. He is a student in the Higher Education doctoral program at the University of Nevada, Las Vegas, and also holds an MLIS degree from Simmons College and an MTS from Harvard University.

JULIANN COUTURE is interdisciplinary social sciences librarian and assistant professor at the University of Colorado Boulder. Her research interests center around studying the student learning experience, and she serves as coordinator for the CU Boulder Libraries' User Experience Working Group.

NANCY FRIED FOSTER facilitates user-centered design through Nancy Foster Design Anthropology, LLC, to help colleges, universities, cultural institutions, and academic libraries develop software, spaces, and services. She served previously as director of anthropological research in the University of Rochester library system and as senior anthropologist at Ithaka S+R. *Studying Students* (coedited with Susan Gibbons) and *The Living Library* (Steele et al.) are among her publications.

BRIAN GREENE is the chief librarian at Columbia College in Sonora, California. His previous community college library experience includes Modesto Junior College in Modesto, California, and Columbia Gorge Community College in The Dalles and Hood River, Oregon. He also worked at academic, public, and special libraries in Seattle while earning an MLIS degree from the University of Washington.

ELIZABETH HORAN is the solo librarian at Coastline Community College in California. Previously she was the distance learning librarian at Saddleback College in California. Her background in digital media has helped support library services for students who access the library off campus or through electronic devices.

DONNA LANCLOS is an anthropologist and folklorist who has been working in academic libraries since 2009 as the associate professor for anthropological research at the J. Murrey Atkins Library at the University of North Carolina, Charlotte. She has conducted research on the academic behaviors of students and professors in the United States and the United Kingdom, and has published her work on the digital and physical places and practices of academia in a variety of venues, including www.donnalanclos.com.

M. SARA LOWE is an associate librarian and educational services librarian at Indiana University-Purdue University Indianapolis. Prior to that, she was an assessment librarian at the Claremont Colleges Library. She has more than ten years of experience with assessment and instruction in academic libraries and has published and presented nationally on topics related to evidence-based librarianship.

WILLIE MILLER has been the informatics and journalism librarian at the University Library of Indiana University-Purdue University Indianapolis since 2010. In addition to subject liaison responsibilities, Miller leads the library's campus outreach initiatives. He has given presentations and published research in the areas of information literacy, instructional technology, library outreach, and space assessment.

PAUL MOFFETT is the head of access services at the University Library of Indiana University-Purdue University Indianapolis, where he oversees a combined service and information desk, stacks management, and building security and emergency planning. His research focuses on the user experience as it relates to service provision and assessment, as well as library space design.

RACHAEL WINTERLING is a user researcher at a financial organization. Previously, she was the usability coordinator and interim head of assessment at the University of North Carolina, Charlotte. She conducts different user experience methodologies such as usability testing, focus groups, interviews, card sorting, surveys, and first click testing. At UNC Charlotte, she used data visualization tools such as Tableau to report qualitative and quantitative data.

TANNER WRAY is director of college libraries and information services at Montgomery College in Maryland, where he is committed to developing and deploying high-quality user-centric services that support student success. He has been involved in ethnographic studies at Montgomery College and at the University of Maryland, where he was director of public services. He has published and presented on his efforts to develop user-centric services at many conferences.

Index

Covit, Raissa, 88
Cowan, Susanna M., 20
CSN
    See College of Southern Nevada
CSN Institutional Research, 118
CSN Libraries, 118
CU Boulder
    See University of Colorado
        Boulder (CU Boulder)
CUNY
    See City University of New York
CUNY OIRA, 69, 71, 78

D

Dace, Karen, 19
Daniels, Erin, 98
data analysis, 88, 108, 109
De Araujo, Pedro, 17
debrief, 20, 21, 25
Deil-Amen, Regina
    on library instruction, 130
    on relationships for information
        networks, 131
    on student/librarian connections, 120
    work on academic libraries/
        student success, 119
Delcore, H. D.
    on commute, 7
    on commuter students, 3, 53
    mapping study for library research, 20
Dembo, Myron H., 118
design
    by architecture students, 109–110
    for future changes at Montgomery
        College Libraries, 114
    participatory design activities by
        library teams, 106–109
    participatory design activities,
        findings from, 110–111
desktop computer, 96
digital divide, 8
distance learning students, 10
distraction, 40, 93
Dominguez, Gricel, 22
"draw your research steps" exercise, 81
drawings
    from CUNY research projects, 75

for ethnographic project, 107, 108
    by students about research project, 72
driving
    See commute
Dryden, Nancy H., 9
Dugan, John P., 2
Duke, Lynda M., 53, 72

E

Eduljee, Nina B., 4, 5
electrical outlets, 63, 64, 113
embedded librarian
    course grade and, 124
    CSN's AIA project to study, 122
    CSN's movement towards, 121
    information literacy/
        confidence and, 127
    results from program, 129
    student engagement and, 128
employment
    See work
engagement
    See student engagement
e-resources, 113
ethnographic project
    outcomes of, 112–115
    research methods for, 106–110
    research question, 104–105
    results of, 110–111
Ethnographic Research in Illinois
    Academic Libraries (ERIAL)
    Project, 72
Evans, Tim, 19

F

faculty
    commuter students, perceptions
        of, 7
    feedback for students, 76
    library instruction and, 120
    technology for contact with
        students, 8
family
    balance between life/school/work, 91
    Family Friendly Library Room, 35–40
    FFLR pre-occupation interviews,
        findings from, 40–42

technology (cont.)
    upgrades at Montgomery College
      Libraries, 112–113
text message survey
    "A Day in the Life" project, 56, 74
    for IUPUI mapping study, 20–21
textbooks
    at Montgomery College Libraries,
      114
    students use of for study, 98–99
time
    commuting, time spent on, 140
    as facilitator/constraint for
      students, 77–79
    lessons learned from commuter
      students, 140
    for student study, 92, 95
    student study habits survey
      responses about, 90–91
Tinto, Vincent, 119, 120
Torres, Vasti, 7
transportation
    commute, research on student
      experience of, 7
    commuter students' college
      experience and, 140
    commuter students, mode
      of transportation, 3
    for CU Boulder students commute
      to/around campus, 59–61
    for CUNY students commute, 78
    use of by students, 10
Twiss-Brooks, Andrea B., 20

U

Undergraduate Scholarly Habits
    Study, 72
University Library (UL) of IUPUI
    conclusions/next steps, 29–30
    institutional context, 19–20
    interventions, 28–29
    mapping study, 20–21
    mapping study, results of, 23–26
    observation study, results of, 26–28
    renovation of, 17
    space needs of, 18
    space study, 21–23

University of Colorado Boulder
    (CU Boulder)
    barriers/frustrations of students, 63
    commute, impact on academic
      work, 61–63
    commute to/around campus, 59–61
    conclusions/next steps for, 65–66
    "A Day in the Life" project, 56
    distances traveled/time spent on
      activities by students, 57–58
    housing, student choice in, 58–59
    institutional context, 54–56
    interventions/initiatives, 64–65
    lessons learned from commuter
      students, 140, 141
    life of students at, 53–54
    mapping/interviews at, 11
University of Colorado Boulder University
    Libraries
    conclusion/next steps, 65–66
    description of, 55–56
    interventions/initiatives, 64–65
    student barriers/frustrations and, 63
    student use of for academic
      work, 61–62
University of Maryland, 104
University of North Carolina, Charlotte
    Atkins Ethnography Project, 34–35
    commuter student at, 1
    conclusion about FFLR, 46–47
    Family Friendly Library Room,
      35–40
    Family Friendly Library Room,
      implementation of, 11
    Family Friendly Library Room,
      partnership for, 141
    institutional context, 33–34
    lessons learned from commuter
      students, 140
    non-users, learning from, 45
    post-occupation interviews,
      findings from, 42–45
    pre-occupation interviews,
      findings from, 40–42
    problem-solving/next steps, 45–46
    research methods for FFLR, 49–51
University of Rochester, 72, 107